Hermit Crab Seeks Home

By Victor Marsh

non-fiction

Mr Isherwood Changes Train:
Christopher Isherwood and the search for the 'home self'

Speak Now:
Australian perspectives on same-sex marriage (editor)

The Boy in the Yellow Dress

poetry

My Teacher's Name is Love

Hermit Crab Seeks Home

Victor Marsh

It is not home that one cries for but one's home-self

Christopher Isherwood

Hear this reed as it complains,
and tells the story of separations.
Ever since I was cut from the reed bed,
My tune made men and women to lament.

Jalal ud-din Rumi, *Masnawi*

rainshadow

© 2025 Victor Marsh

ISBN: 978-1-7637356-6-8 (paperback)

Published by rainshadow, an imprint of Clouds of Magellan Press, Melbourne.

www.cloudsofmagellanpress.net

All rights reserved. No part of this publication may be reproduced without permission of the author.

Design: Gordon Thompson
Cover image: Balthasar van der Ast. Wikimedia Commons

Contents

Introduction   vii

1

Living in La-la Land

Shakedown	3
Dress ups	8
Learning how to be gay	16
Yes, I *choose!*	24
Testing the limits	33
Coming out, spiritually	35
Two-spirit	38
City of (lost) angels (i)	46
Meetings with remarkable women (i)	48
Civic unrest	60
City of (lost) angels (ii)	67
Hustled!	68
Postcards from the edge	75
Meetings with remarkable women (cont.)	83
Tracking down that damned elusive boson	85
Shingles (or, crocodile skin?)	92
Unsettled	96

2

Back in the Land of Oz

Love in taxis	101
Welcome home!	106
New land, old land	110
Deluge	118
A different kind of strength	125
Notes for a journal of awakening	131
Error of parallax	141
Breakthrough (Psyche's wisdom)	143
Out Uluru way …	147

The power of listening	152
Close encounters	157
Rapprochement	164
Come as you are	166
'Coming out' as a 'spiritual' portal	167
Crashing the printer	173
Out of my way	176
Transitions	179
Magpie's song	182
Transitions of another kind	186
Acceptance	191
Choosing love	193
Perth	197
Snow on the roof	202
Could this be love?	209
Full circle	212

Acknowledgements
Bibliography

Introduction

An earlier memoir, *The Boy in the Yellow Dress*, began at the age of around three or four years. Here I pick up the narrative well into the 'Hollywood years', aged around forty-nine. To recap: I'm travelling in a 1945 Model body/brain, having been born in Perth, Western Australia, where I did a lot of theatre at Uni and beyond into my early twenties. I suffered from a feeling of suffocation in my home state and sought oxygen by running away for more than fifty years, travelling through the idealistic counterculture as an acolyte of the hippie revolution and the anti-war resistance movement. After an earnest engagement with psychedelic drugs (my favourite was mescaline) and reading a lot of books that delved into comparative religion and new forms of spirituality, in my late twenties I met a young Teacher, and I served for several years as a travelling meditation instructor on his behalf.

I gave that work my best shot but after eleven years I realised that I was not able to live up to the rigours of the lifestyle required to maintain the required level of self-discipline, especially the requirement of celibacy, as a (modern-day) monk. While that strictly focused life had been a huge relief to me initially, wrestling as I was with issues to do with gender and sexuality, towards the end of that cycle of renunciation I felt compelled to seek out a better option than denial of sexuality altogether.

However, I had certainly experienced the pragmatic benefits of regular meditation practice and, rather than throwing the baby out with the proverbial bathwater, I have continued with the practice through all the ups and downs that have ensued as I shifted into a (radically) different lifestyle. Moreover, while I saw this as taking a step 'backwards', in a sense, the ongoing guidance of my Teacher has continued to deepen and benefit me in ways I can scarcely describe, even as I pursued work in TV production, which is where I landed from around age 38 ... So, after giving up trying to be a monk, I took jobs in television, initially in Melbourne and Sydney, and then on to the U.S.)

The most recent of these, a science and technology show called *Beyond 2000*, has brought me to Los Angeles ...

1

Living in La-la Land

Shakedown

January 17th, 1994. Hollywood, California

Two old friends from Melbourne are in town and they take me out to dinner. This is a real treat for me, beyond what my spartan budget usually allows. Paul and Elaine like to put away a glass or three of red wine and I drink more during dinner than I'm accustomed to. Afterwards, I return to my studio apartment, where I sit to meditate before sleeping.

This remains part of my normal practice, even years after leaving the ashrams, where I used to reside. But I don't like to meditate while tipsy and, before I sit, I perform a little home-made ritual, something I haven't done for decades. I light some choice incense, formally offering it up to all the points of the compass, requesting the protection and guidance of all the Buddhas and Enlightened Beings, in every direction, on every plane. My meditation is a little woozy and I crawl into bed around 2.00 am.

4.31 am

I'm awoken abruptly, with my queen-size bed jumping and thumping about in the dark. The street lighting, which is usually on all night, disappears completely and we're plunged into deep blackness. Random crashing sounds punctuate the dark as the rocking continues. This neighbourhood is densely populated, and every car alarm bleats, screams and whoops. The discombobulation continues, as the intense rattling and shaking extends into protracted time. How long will this last?

Half a minute, I learn later … Long enough for a good shake-up.

I'm wide awake and out of bed now, but cautious not to run in the darkness. According to the regular community service announcements on TV we should have placed rubber-soled shoes by our beds to be at hand (or foot?) in the event of emergencies. Where are they now? And where's that bloody flashlight when I need it?

I'm trying to think clearly; but I'm on edge. Anything I'm trying to hold onto is moving.

When did I last replace the gallon containers of water? 'Enough to supply all your needs for drinking, bathing, washing and cooking for at least three days' is the oft-repeated advice from the public service announcements. There are two or three ten-gallon bottles under the sink in the kitchen. And you might need some water bottles in the car too. No, I haven't done that. What if I have to get the car out of the underground garage … will the door open? The gate is electrically operated.

And where am I thinking to go, in any case?

I find my flashlight, check the floor and scan the apartment for signs of damage. In spite of the radical shake-up, it seems there isn't any structural damage. In the kitchen, a glass has fallen into the sink, where it has broken safely. A soft lamp has tipped to its side, unharmed, and my bronze Buddha statue has fallen sideways, dinging his halo.

I'd laugh, but I'm not insensitive to the synchronicity and I've learned that such events typically serve as a kind of wake-up call, a peculiar kind of attentiveness which may not last …

Just as I start to calm down, an aftershock whacks us around again. There'll be no going back to sleep this morning …

Tremors are common in most parts of California. I haven't experienced them growing up and until now I've perversely found the movements curiously interesting – even a little entertaining. You just don't expect the one thing you take for granted – that the ground under your feet will remain stable – to suddenly and drastically overturn your cosy, unconscious assumptions in such a radical shift. Here in LA my friends, who have learned to fear the destructive potential of even the smallest, barely detectable tremble, have not shared my perverse enjoyment.

While such reminders tend to create a pause in normal activity, it's usually short-lived, as we all do an almost subliminal scan to sense if it's going to continue, or even strengthen, before normal activity resumes. After this day, perhaps I'll have learned a little more respect and I won't mention it with mockery anymore.

Over the next few hours news trickles in, at first via radio then, surprisingly quickly, even on television. Live 'crosses' to the earthquake centre in Pasadena focus on the seismograph needle that has traced the sudden jolt. They are reporting something like a magnitude 6.7, later revised up a point as a 6.8, and then down again. Numerous smaller but noticeable aftershocks ripple through the remainder of the day.

The epicentre is in the San Fernando Valley. Puzzled geophysicists report that the event has been triggered by a previously unidentified fault among a tangle of deep irregularities under the Los Angeles basin. Others, connected, go through minor rupturing during the main shock. I've heard about the big San Andreas Fault of course, that runs up California, but that's out in the desert, inland – we've even done stories on that, and the much feared coming BIG ONE, on *Beyond 2000*, the TV show I'm working on – but this web of deep smaller faults under Los Angeles is still only partially mapped.

They're reporting that a section of freeway overpass, the 10 East/West, has collapsed onto La Cienega. The 10 is crucial to traffic flow across to the 405, with its north/south connection to the main airport. Sections of buildings on old parts of Hollywood Boulevard, just two blocks north and a little east of my apartment, will be declared unsafe. And to the West, beach side Santa Monica itself has been shaken up.

I hear reports of the first casualty: in the darkness, a Highway Patrolman out in San Bernardino, who leapt onto his motorbike to report for duty, has driven over the edge of another section of collapsed freeway, in the dark, and fallen to his death. There are no other reports of casualties … yet. Commentators suggest that the early hour has meant there was little traffic. It's also a partial public holiday, commemorating Martin Luther King, so fewer people were going about their business.

Near the original epicentre out in Northridge, in the San Fernando Valley, serious structural damage has collapsed some apartment buildings like concertinas, and one has killed 16 people.

Reports of deaths will pile up over the next day or two, from 57 up to 60, while more than 8,000 people will be reported injured.

A couple of hours later I manage to contact Paul and Elaine at their hotel in West Hollywood. Elaine spent some years in school in California when she was very young, and the shake-up has provoked a strong anxiety reaction, reminding her of the drills they had to practise regularly in her classrooms.

It's hard to switch off the weird sense of excitement, now intermingled with relief, and my own body remains on alert. Attention is fragmented but, even as the stress hormones begin to clear from the bloodstream, the series of aftershocks – two in the range of a Richter 6 – provoke a new cycle of tension; so I don't really get to relax. While these bursts of heightened stress make me feel physically weary, I continue to check the news reports obsessively for updates.

I thread my way across the couple of miles to pick up my friends and bring them to my flat. While we wait out the news, I come to their aid with pots of calming camomile tea. The airport was closed immediately after the main event but by evening we manage to get them onto a flight out.

I've noticed that the quakes and temblors have different motions. One morning I was lying awake in the early light and watching with interest as all the straight, vertical lines of walls and furniture trembled and wavered. On other occasions it's a simple shaking and with others, it's a distinct jolt, like a very large truck has crashed into the foundations.

This one, the so-called Northridge quake of January 1994, is centred near Reseda. It's classified as a 'blind thrust' type, that has rumbled up from a depth of about 11.4 miles and was felt as far away as Las Vegas. One of the two size 6 aftershocks occurred very soon after the initial event, and the second around 11 hours later.

I am by now hyper-sensitised to the smaller activity that rumbles between these events.

Other interconnected faults have ruptured, and I will learn new respect for the jelly-like mysteries of the LA basin as it inexorably squeezes up into the San Bernardino mountains.

There's probably nowhere in the world where earthquake activity is so closely studied as in California and building codes have been re-jigged again and again as the geophysics is better understood. An event like this will cause revisions to the codes. In fact a major upgrade of some freeways is already underway, following the devastating event up north in San Francisco in 1989, not long after I arrived to work here in the south of the state. That one sandwiched layers of freeways onto each other, crushing cars between them, and broke the upper layer of the bridge across the Bay to Oakland. But that required a huge infrastructure upgrade and not all of the many overpasses scheduled for re-building up and down the State have yet received funding.

Once again, the whole state is on edge.

During the post-event analyses I note ruefully that most casualties and damage down here in the south, where I am located, occurred in multi-story, wooden frame buildings. In particular, buildings with an unstable first floor (such as those with parking areas on the bottom, like mine!) nearer the epicentre, are reported to have performed poorly.

I'm still puzzled by my little incense ritual; just why that came to mind and why I was prompted to perform it, just hours before the shakedown! Was my little quasi-prayer ritual effective in protecting me from harm?

The shifts in underlying geology are like a virtual prelude to a series of other kinds of shake-ups, not restricted to goings on in the material world, as I soon discover. Some of them come from my own innate curiosity, some in the troubled realm of racial politics, on the external level, but it is becoming clear that my world-mapping needs some radical revisioning, on more levels than I could have predicted. Somehow, even while dealing with the demands of a job and all that entails, my so-called 'spiritual' journey will not be totally interrupted.

Dress ups

Beverly Hills

It's late October. There's a nip in the air, even if the sky outside is clear. I'm ensconced in the chair of a chic make-up salon in Beverly Hills, having splurged on a professional make-over before the street party in West Hollywood this evening. I've brought my costume along so Paula will get the colour palette right – tones of amethyst, plum and black. Black because it's Halloween, which always incorporates an element of the dead coming back to life.

I'm going as a dead bride.

I located a shop on Melrose that sells used bridal wear. None of the actual bridal gowns (all white) fitted me. Like it or not, I am better fitted to the mother-of-the-bride end of the range, but I found a matron-of-honour (or perhaps a mother–of-the-bride) two-piece with a top layer of lace over a satin skirt. *Pink!* That would never do. This top has batwing sleeves, cleverly cut for the generous proportions of a woman of a certain age.

Even in the larger sizes it's difficult to find a dress that can accommodate male shoulders, so I'm chuffed that the space allowed for a large bosom in its original incarnation makes way for my broader torso. The elegant skirt is longer at the back than the front and has a fetching kick to it.

I've borrowed a pair of low black heels from an acquaintance more accustomed to 'cross-dressing' for fun. Even in Richard's low heels, I'll have to rehearse walking carefully, to avoid snagging the lace train. I could never be a 'drag queen'; it's too damned fussy. Once a year is enough for me, at Halloween.

To render the pink in a more sombre hue, I dye the ensemble, commandeering one of the washing machines in the laundry room of my apartment building, using a mixture of purple and black dyes. It ends up as a cross between tea-rose and mulberry, and the different layers of fabric have taken up the colour in some lovely ways I couldn't have predicted.

A costumier who lives across the hall in my Hollywood apartment building has agreed to make my veil. Marcy does wardrobe for period dramas on television, like *Doctor Quinn, Medicine Woman*. You just never know who your neighbours will be in Tinseltown.

'It'll be easy,' Marcy assures me. 'Just pick up six yards of black tulle from that store on Beverley and I'll stitch it in place for you in no time.' I've already plundered her collection of antique jewellery to find the perfect jet choker.

The outfit has been coming together with a certain synchronous grace, right down to the accessories.

For my six yards of tulle I made a pilgrimage to International Silks and Woolens (that's how they spell it here) on Beverly Boulevard, like every other queen in LA prepping for All Hallows Eve (Halloween, or Samhain, to the Celts, celebrating the onset of winter, and given an extra twist here in queer West Hollywood). The boundary between the worlds of the living and the dead is beginning to blur.

Behind the counters, women of a certain age from Russia, Persia and other old-world backgrounds are tickled pink by the parade of men who come into the store for supplies. For weeks beforehand, muscle-bound gym bunnies have agonized over lynx-print stretch fabrics, with others trying out various degrees of sparkling brilliance.

Every wannabe designer moves to LA to get into 'the industry', and, as most of the men are gay, the outfits for this celebration will be simply stunning.

I'm a tad too lazy to start from scratch, but my outfit, made up from found *objets*, will give them a run for their money. The shop assistants conspire with subtle smiles, sharing in the triumph of finding the right glittering fabric for the outrageous outfits coming together for our night out on the town. Many of these women from various cultural backgrounds will join the large crowd drawn out to view the passing parade on Santa Monica Boulevard in WeHo Boys' Town, West Hollywood, where the sheriffs close down several blocks of the Boulevard to allow the party relatively free rein. It's like Carnaval in Rio, or a Masked Ball in Venice, and in this part of town it's totally gay.

'Tell me about her,' Paula says as she riffles through her supplies. 'What kind of mood are you trying to create?'

'Well, she was jilted and left at the altar, poor soul. She never removed her bridal gown and just kind of faded away.'

'Like that old lady in …?'

'… *Great Expectations*, that's the one. But I don't want her looking too decrepit. The dye-job turned out too well for that.'

The costume has started to shape the character. My fantasy bride will be Miss Havisham before the rot set in, and elegantly dressed by say, Schiaparelli.

'Did you bring the wig?'

I nod. 'You have to imagine her face shaded by a black tulle veil. That will go on last. I think she would be quite pale in complexion, with doleful eyes.'

Paula and I have taken off early from the TV show where we both work and she has booked me a session in her private boutique off Dayton Way. Paula is one of the best in the biz., and her studio is a small but elegant space where she meets private clients after hours. Each piece of furniture stands alone for maximum minimalist effect and small halogen pin-spots highlight the colour on the walls, which has been ragged, or sponged for a textured effect. The floor is polished painted concrete with a well-chosen rug or two.

'Let me just clean these up a little,' she says, attacking my raggedy eyebrows with a pair of tweezers.

I've already shaved off the moustache but, as a real part-timer in the drag stakes, I draw the line at any more invasive depilations. I'll cover my legs with the black lace hosiery I wore last year and, if I wear the elbow-length black gloves, I won't need to shave my arms, or deal with unnecessary complications such as stick-on nails. Besides, who needs talons? I'm not going as a witch; I've done that before. This time I'll be a real lady, a *tragédienne* trailing her sorrows in the dust, intoning a melancholy lay of lost love and betrayal along the boulevard of broken dreams.

She'll have to look pretty good to hold her own among the superb outfits swanning around, so a song will be sure to snag some attention. I've borrowed mine from the music hall era and I plan to perform it impromptu to audiences from among the throng of onlookers.

As a final touch, I've asked a florist to make up a wedding bouquet of red roses and bake it in an oven so that the flowers are scorched. And I've trimmed it with a trail of black and purple ribbons.

Back at the apartment, Marcy is building the tulle veil over an antique headdress that I've found and she's working out how to secure it to the black wig that will cover my bald head. I'll wrap an elasticized bandage around my skull and hook the wig securely into that so it doesn't slide off (a little trick I learned in my theatre days). The crowds on the boulevard can be brutal.

'Why a dead bride?' Paula asks as she daubs on foundation over a layer of moisturizer. 'This will give a good foundation to even out the surface of your skin. It's not too pale is it?'

'Well, it's Halloween – you know that brief window in time when the spirits of the departed walk among the living. Time to let the black cat out of the bag, so to speak.' That's the usual explanation but, to my experimentally Jungian mindset, what has been suppressed or pushed down into the shadow side of the psyche, if you like, is allowed out to play. All the things we fear about ourselves come out of hiding. Perhaps it does have something to do with archetypes, if I understood Jung a little better.

Little do I know what forces I'm playing with.

'Do you do this very often?' She's dabbing foundation into the corner of my eye-sockets.

'What? The drag thing? No, as a matter of fact, until recently I hadn't done it – dressed up, that is – for… let me see, it must have been nearly fifty years. You must understand, this is a departure from my normal sobriety. Personally, I often find drag queens a little gaudy…'

Paula is amused.

I've been queer for as long as I can remember, but I had never gone in for the drag scene. They don't do Halloween in Australia, where I grew up. And for me, it's never been about trying to become a girl. My father died a couple of years ago. After his funeral I found a photo in a family album and it reminded me of something I used to do when I was a very little boy: the incident with the iconic yellow dress.

'Do you need the eyelashes now?' I ask.

'You brought your own? O.K. I have some better adhesive than that, though.' Thank God she's doing the eyelashes. Last year I nearly blinded myself.

As Paula works her magic, I remember reading how the Kathakali dancers of South India go into a trance while assistants slowly apply their make-up, preparing to become possessed by the characters they are to play in their marathon, all-night performances. I welcome the entrance of my alter ego as she gathers together her props and prepares for her brilliant, if rare, nocturnal outing. Even without my glasses I can see that Paula has caught the spirit perfectly.

Although I'm in full make-up, a lingering sense of decorum makes me aware that passers-by might find me a trifle odd – fully made up, but in civilian clothes – and, as I make my way back to the car-park on Bedford, I virtually will onlookers to direct their gaze towards the costume I'm carrying just so that there's no misunderstanding.

'See? It's Halloween, and this is my costume!'

In secret, a shift is occurring, almost like a drug coming on. I know that such temporary discretion will be displaced by the rising tide of confidence that will nudge aside the shallow divisions of 'normal' reality. A spirit of joy will infect everyone with whom it comes into contact. Tonight, we shall dance.

Much later, in the early morning hours, as I peel out of the costume and remove the make-up, a memory tugs for my closer attention. I lie down, relieved to be off my feet, exhausted by the effort of walking in heels and the constant struggle to keep my tulle veil from snagging on passersby. Brief images from the party on the Boulevard wash over my mind's eye – I did have my picture taken with an amused West Hollywood Sheriff, and I remember a young Latino guy feeling under my dress to check out my 'real' gender – but an insistent older memory rises up for review and I let that come through. When I first dressed in a woman's gown, aged three or four, and I was taught to be ashamed. I have only recently realised, decades since, that my parents' confiscation of the dress was a grossly inappropriate response to what was going on in the psyche of a young child.

So, what is it about this gender play that feels so joyful now? I think it is something of the same order that occurs in the 'coming out' process for us queer folk. There's a release of some kind of psychic energy that is usually bottled up as we deal with suppression and denial; but this feels distinctly like joy; a restitution of the natural ordering of identity, liberated from the narrow, toxic constructions of mean-spirited types inclined to react suspiciously towards anything that feels like joy, in fact.

As I see it, it's about a re-awakening of dormant neural pathways that enable intelligence to seek out new dimensions of awareness shut down ordinarily by conventional thinking.

Some people reading this material might be thinking: Why is this guy so bothered by these issues? Has he really been persecuted so badly? Times have changed!

But the long-term damage of shaming, however and wherever it occurs, has a deeply divisive effect not only within an individual psyche but on the whole society, when people are encouraged (or coerced) to shut down their innate expression of creativity and joy, especially where it is negatively sanctioned by people who speak for 'God'. Shame is a blunt tool used by the agents of conformity to coerce deviants to fit themselves into the narrow conventions of 'normal' society, that Procrustean iron bed of Greek legend. If it don't fit, amputate!

In my experience, the much touted 'Gay pride' will always be rootless, even false, for me unless I have dealt with the internalised sense of shame. Perhaps it's not so much about 'coming out' but of coming 'in' to deal with the effects of internalised homophobia. And then, events like this may indeed feel like a celebration.

I often wonder how women used to undergo virtual torture, squeezing their bodies into whalebone corsets to attain an ideal shape for the male gaze and perhaps even for each other; and how in China, upper-class girls' feet were crushed from infancy because the prevailing aesthetics of the male gaze sexualised tiny feet, causing great suffering, long-term. Broad feet on women were peasants' feet.

In a piece he wrote for my sister when she was constructing a family history for a course that she was studying, my father described how he was hobbled by early 20th century attitudes which viewed him as 'illegitimate'– a child born 'out of wedlock'. In his own words:

Illegitimacy, when I became aware of it in my early years, was a handicap, a stigma, a sword of Damocles hanging over my head, & when I thought it was forgotten, would occasionally spring up and bug me. It prevented me, at one stage, applying for a job in the State Government.

I am really pleased to read Australian scholar Rosamund Dalziell, then, who has written about the issue of shame in contemporary writing, explaining how shaming is related to *an exercise of power* whereby 'the economically and socially powerful maintain a 'discourse of respectability' by shaming those who did not conform to their mores.

Dalziell writes that 'the confessional origins of autobiography as a literary genre lend themselves to the revelation of hidden and shameful aspects of the self.' [Dalziell. 132] She focused specifically on the shaming related to the issue of 'illegitimacy' of birth and writes that 'marginalised and unauthorised discourse ... holds the power to *disrupt* authorised versions of experience, even, perhaps to reveal what might be called the randomness and arbitrariness of the authoritative and public constructs of reality.' [p. 136]

This is a challenge that my father faced throughout his life, and I consider it now as part of a karmic, intergenerational issue, which both me and my Dad have had to deal with, in different ways.

For me, writing autobiographically becomes a resistant strategy for writing (and discovering) my identity, shifting past the binary boundaries; providing the opportunity to assert a reframed version of self; finding out what I feel about the peculiar person I am discovering myself to be; taking control of stereotyped meanings away from the toxic characterisations embedded within discourses controlled by forces not well-disposed to social mis-behaviour. By using this assertive strategy, as the 'subject' created by these hostile forces, I become an agent of self-signification.

Maybe some will take this as an unhealthy preoccupation, but I will go on to take this work further, to show how other areas of experience considered out of bounds for queer folk – particularly, in my case, the religious life – can also be reclaimed by this dissident narrative practice.

And the gleanings of meaning will open me up to an enhanced awareness of being here, in this world, with other people.

As I learn, post-earthquake, to fool with the stifling constructions of gender, I will come to understand what potentials of consciousness are blocked off by fitting into these suffocating, corset-like conventions, no matter how widely they are followed, nor what toxic instruments of morality hold sway over the public moral imaginary, and why.

Instinctively, my lifelong research has focused on the liberation of queer folk (namely me!) from oppressive representations of identity tethered to sexuality and certain psycho-pathological notions of a failure along developmental pathways still privileged as 'normal'.

I am not satisfied with the role of conventional religions in producing a pariah caste through their typical constructions that thrive on 'the violence of exclusion' and would cheat us queer folk from developing our full potential; a potential that I find is envisioned more positively in models from other cultures not dependent on typically toxic, homophobic narratives. By rejecting the mean-spirited constructions that serve to ensure a crude conformity, perhaps we might demonstrate a way to greater freedom for them, too, as they struggle against imported cultural models.

But I'm not waiting for others to find peace or develop a more authentic selfhood. I am emerging from a chrysalis and gradually gathering energy to breakthrough, now!

This is an instinctive process because the urge has not, especially in my early years, received support from authority figures. When I encounter authentically deep thinkers like the great psychoanalyst Carl Jung, I begin to recognise that the publicly approved models of identity that do not support my growing sense of self might just be hollow after all, and not at all life-sustaining:

> In the same way that the body needs food, and not just any kind of food but only that which suits it, the psyche needs to know the meaning of its existence – not just any meaning, but the meaning of those images and ideas which reflect its nature and which originate in the Unconscious.
> [Jung, *Collected Works*, Vol. 13, par. 476]

Learning how to be gay

West Hollywood

With my alleged 'love life' on a more or less continual, if unwilling hold, I have to admit to myself that there seems to be some kind of block. (I should have kissed enough frogs by now to find my prince.)

The bars are of no avail. I've never really enjoyed drinking – apart from a good French champagne, when I can afford it – and can't relax in those all-male settings, gay or not-gay. Perhaps it reminds me too much of some of my father's clubs. I am impatient with all the sitting around, getting drunk, when what everyone is really hoping for is to connect. Because of my advanced age – I'm already past my mid-forties – people assume that I ought to have money, but I'm still living on the parsimonious salary disbursed by my Australian employers, so I'd be hard pushed to pay my way to ersatz forms of intimacy and affection.

Which is not to say that I have given up the 'ghost' in this regard. If 'hope springs eternal in the human breast' it continues to show hopeful signs in other parts of my human anatomy.

'Just go along at closing time, sometime after 2 am', advises my friend Cliff. 'At that time of night, people don't care who they go home with.'

That's the problem. Unfortunately, I do care whom I go home with! And dancing by myself in the disco venues is becoming a little tragic. It's good aerobic exercise yes, but for someone my age, it lacks a little dignity. Someone should advise me to 'act my age', which my close friend and advisor Susan occasionally does (notably ignoring her own advice with a couple of younger men with whom she hooks up).

And I know I carry the solution, at least potentially.

I drive out to Malibu for screenings of videos of talks given by my blessed (and very modern) Teacher. I've known him since I was 27 (and he was 14). For months, the theme he reiterates in these videos, is: 'What you are looking for can only be found within.'

In my internal dialogue I tend to bat this advice aside: 'Yes I know. I got the message. I do the meditation practices every day and have been doing so for many years. I tried the focused monastic lifestyle for nigh-on eleven years, but I am no longer trying to be a monk. I left the ashram so I might stroke silky skin, guilt-free.'

Repeat: 'What you are looking for can only be found within.'

Yes, it's inside. I know that. That's why I continue with the meditation practices every day. *But where's the boyfriend?* I gave myself permission to play more when I gave up living as a monk, but 'the Universe' seems to want to be withholding this kind of pleasure. Other people manage to find a partner, why not me?

If you pray to a 'God' and 'He' doesn't come through, *maybe He's saying no?* I push that thought down.

Eventually the message starts to seep through my thick skull, 'Oh! He is actually talking to me' … *and he's pointedly addressing my situation.*

Is my queer nature not really about sex after all?

It seems that I tend to do things full bore, or not at all, and many times the most abrupt changes in my life, while baffling even to me at the time, open up long arcs of discovery. Leaving Helm, my first love, and getting away from Perth to go to grad. school in Sydney; going to Melbourne after the big LSD shakedown; leaving my partner to go into the ashram; then leaving that, eleven years later and getting into television; moving from Sydney to Los Angeles on just a few days' notice, and so on … Each time it could have seemed like a form of self-sabotage, but each situation (and its challenges) has opened up major new discoveries.

As part of that I am pushed to re-examine the gay issue again and again. When I was living with the mother of my child, I was hoping to change my 'orientation' and I was radically unsettled when it didn't work. The ashram beckoned, and celibacy looked like a healthy alternative for someone so ready to wreak havoc in others' lives. I wasn't reading much about gay lib. when I was in the exclusively focused world of the ashram, but that type of 'liberation' movement, as a sign of a major shift in the collective unconscious, certainly didn't leave me unaffected. Yes, I wanted to get laid (and not feel guilty about it). But more than that, I had to find out just how real this gendered sexuality issue was. Has this all been delusional? Was I just going back into 'worldly' living to pick away endlessly at the wound?

I struggle for months to find someone with whom to play the game of love and then I give up again to lie, defeated. With my inner ear resting in the pillow of the breath, I listen to my heart breathing songs of praise and gratitude, surrendering to a spontaneous meditation. And I find rest – asleep awake, awake asleep – drifting quietly through states of bliss, recognizing where home ultimately is … And wrench myself away again, on cycles of rebellion and disquiet, desperately trying to reconstruct reality according to my own desires.

My Teacher Prem (May He forgive me for my waywardness!) says that a wild bird captured and caged too long will sometimes not fly away and gain its freedom again when the cage door is opened!

But it's getting used to being gay, or more exactly, 'queer'. That sad and happy misery has bent and twisted and writhed within me, again and again insisting on my attentions, for as long as I can recall. I've tried to resist it, with a decade of formal celibacy to release me from the grip of sexuality altogether. Who is a 'homosexual' when he's not having sex? Is sexuality a reliable basis for constructing an identity?

It may not be ultimate reality; does the 'soul', my essential being, have a gender, after all? By the grace of my Teacher and 25 years of fairly consistent practice, I have felt my roots all the way back to that ultimate reality where all is one. I can't deny that.

Among the myths from ancient Greece, Ariadne left a thread for her lover Theseus to find his way out of the labyrinth after slaughtering the Bull, saving his life in the process. The Goddess has left her subtle signal for me, concealed within my breath, to recover my way back to life. But in the world of relativity, variables, the finite, the particulars, there are a *multiplicity* of identities to live out.

It seems that I must find a way to face this being gay/queer/whatever, and my dharma seems to be inextricably woven into resolving that apparent dilemma and weaving it into the context of a sacred matrix that I am still learning to accept, wholeheartedly. Access to the infinite, after years of being shut out by ignorance and shame, has been the basis for my healing process, my wholeness. My Teacher is patient with me as I wrestle with my issues and his meditation practices are a blessing and a true balm.

I am starting to risk the idea that to be 'gay' might just be a gift, like so many other things this world rejects. So, I will continue to probe its meaning, heal the division, and allow it to be incorporated, somehow, into a new sense of wholeness.

1992

My ears tickle when I hear of the formation of a new institute, based in West Hollywood. It's to be called The Institute of Gay and Lesbian Education, or IGLE, and all the courses will be taught by gay and lesbian professors drawn from among the many campuses of the various colleges and universities around Southern California.

Signs of intelligent life in Boystown! At last, an alternative to the discos, bars and beats. Perhaps here I'll meet someone more suitable here than the disco dancers, who are not attracted to me anyway.

There's a rumour that it was to have been called the West Hollywood Institute for Gay and Lesbian Education (hence the acronym 'WHIGLE') but it is alleged (perhaps unfairly) that the lesbians on the faculty found that acronym too 'lightweight'.

Nonetheless, over the next two years semester-long courses on offer will include studies in the biology of sexuality, gay-affirmative psychology, sexual ethics, gay & lesbian lit., creative writing workshops, and more.

The convenor and prime mover of the Institute is Dr Simon LeVay, a noted British neuroscientist, and his own course on 'sexual dimorphism in the human brain' is informed by his own scientific research. During a career in brain studies Simon has discovered that a particular part of the brain appears to be differently formed in gay men.

Naturally, the research is already causing controversy but is enthusiastically received by those of us interested in finding a way through to more contemporary constructions of morality that ring true to us.

Each year, as a representative of *Beyond 2000* I attend an international conference of new scientific research, in different US cities. I'm talking with a British science writer, who surprises me with his scepticism on such matters, so it appears the possibility has not won widespread credibility. Snide remarks have been circulating among sceptics in the wider community: 'So, you have to learn how to be gay now, do you?'

That's not how I see it. To understand my own situation is a driving force that must be appeased. I'm sick of being identified as a 'sexual orientation' and represented that way by forces hostile to my fulfilment. There's got to be some better way to understand the challenge of being me in this particular time and space. Perhaps this discomfort will eventually, oyster-like, produce a pearl.

Some birds can plunge into water to seize their prey and they emerge fully able to fly away. Others cannot do that because their feathers are soaked with water. What's the difference between these species? One type secretes an oil that coats its feathers so that the water does not disempower them. And what is it in my make-up that protects me from these toxic forces? It's not as if I am deaf to the slander from all sides – religious pariah, social misfit, psychopathological specimen – compounded with the fear of a poorly imagined 'God' figure who does not, allegedly, love all of His Creation.

The work I have been doing, with my Teacher's guidance, for at least a quarter of a century now, has been healing me from within. There is something more to me than my desires; something that is recovered whole in the connection with an indwelling reality. As an experience, not an idea.

If I do 'follow' a religion, it's 'religion' in its original sense. To be bound together with the force that sustains my very breath. Recovering the presence of the power that makes my life possible, from breath to sacred breath. Commune with that, at the root of being, and relinquish all other facsimiles.

In LA, the Press have been alerted and, on the day of the Institute's official opening, CNN will send a crew along to cover the event. On this day in Hollywood, the dream factory par excellence, I start my morning by tuning in to this fundamental order of Reality; from the inside, in meditation. And I visualise myself speaking confidently on TV.

I 'power dress' and spend my working day in a state of calm, if alert, expectation. After work, I drive over to the IGLE rooms in West Hollywood, arriving just as CNN is setting up to record some interviews.

As I walk through the door, the camera swings my way and, walking towards me, the field producer throws out the question: 'What do you hope to learn by studying here?'

Another force – a certainty rather than self-doubt – prevails within me. And I respond: 'Knowledge is power. The understanding I gain here turns back the ignorance of those who want to persecute me.' (I try to keep it simple. With my experience in TV production, I know they'll use only a short soundbite.)

A day or two later, I notice that the impressive Elizabeth Taylor, a pioneer in promoting respect towards gay people in Hollywood, uses the same line in a TV interview: 'Knowledge is power.'

June 1995

After two years of after-hours study at IGLE I graduate with another chap (wearing rainbow-striped mortar boards and borrowed academic gowns), with a Diploma in Gay and Lesbian Studies, and I'm rather pleased with myself. If only they could see me now, I think to myself, as I recall that other time when I graduated, with my parents standing alongside, politely eating white bread sandwiches with the crusts trimmed off, in Perth, in 1967.

This certificate means more to me than that Bachelor of Arts degree (with first class honours nonetheless!) and it has more direct relevance to my real life now. People like me have existed right throughout various periods in history. Reading that history is something I can take seriously, and personally.

At the ceremony, I read a short memoir piece I penned during one of the writing workshops – the one about my white rabbit giving birth to a litter of kittens of different colours, some twenty-eight days after her trembling conjunction with an equally white buck – and I revel in presenting the end line: 'I still know little about genetics, but I do know that two parents can produce offspring quite unlike them in many ways.'

The fact that my fellow graduates' parents are at the ceremony make my conclusion a little edgier than I might have planned.

At the next Gay Pride parade through West Hollywood, we ride down Santa Monica Boulevard in the back of an open-air limousine, waving to the crowds. I don't know if there will be a boost in enrolments. Maybe they'd be happier in the discos? So be it. I got what I came here for, a healthier and more affirmative sense of selfhood. (And the effects of meditation temper an unstable 'Pride'.)

The wider society seemingly remains inoculated against these nascent signs of assertiveness. Newly elected President Clinton suffers a defeat early in his first term in office, when he faces his first major challenge over the thorny issue of 'gays in the military'. The resulting compromise – a policy to be known as 'Don't Ask, Don't Tell' – results in a worse situation for my people caught in that bind, with ongoing reports of a more active imperative to hunt us down and discharge us.

But the political struggle will continue on other fronts. The current model of identity formation holds that identity emerges exclusively within a social context and that our relations with others are essential to the formation of the self, so the dissident irruptions such as 'coming out of the closet' are a marked change from one's usual shrinking posture. For, as it has been said, 'shame hides its head'. In effect, as an inner rather than physical wound, shaming can always operate to divide us against ourselves.

I know that the suicide rate is higher among gay teenagers. I recognise their pain and I mourn their passing. Suicide is at the extreme edge of a range of forms of self-harm. Later still, I will read about the theories of the French philosopher Michel Foucault about how social control needs to be 'internalised' in order that obedient subjects of society can be relied on to, in effect, police their own behaviour. Psychologically speaking, if the roots of shame haven't been addressed in the personal psyche, that behaviour (often compulsive, addictive) rooted in the unexplored unconscious mind can control conscious behaviour, overwhelming the conscious rationalisations and, ultimately, may result in behaviours that surprise or confuse a depressed person.

At IGLE we gather courage from each other's example. During a stimulating unit of study on the ethics of sexuality, I am encouraged by the probing of outstanding moral philosophers like Richard D. Mohr and John Corvino and a number of women, way ahead of us, who convincingly challenge the underpinnings of lazy prejudices that have held sway, largely unchallenged, for what seems like centuries.

Work stemming from serious research into the biology of human sexuality by Dean Hamer at UCLA, and notably by the founder of IGLE himself, the British neuroscientist Simon LeVay who is now residing in West Hollywood, are also shaking up the bases of unexamined prejudice. I feel hope for a renovated education system that will open itself to new streams of knowledge, rather than reiterating lazy versions of reality.

Meanwhile at nearby Fairfax high school, a wise and courageous teacher named Dr. Virginia Uribe pioneers a 'safe space' project for queer kids to find shelter at school from bullying and harassment. Virginia has started a gay/straight alliance called 'Project 10', the first dropout prevention program specifically for lesbian, gay, bisexual and transgender students in the US, in 1988.

Predictably, the public protests against Dr. Uribe's work have been spear-headed by Lou Sheldon, a Baptist pastor who runs what he calls the Traditional Values Coalition, which lobbies for traditional, conservative Christian values. He gets lots of Press. Virginia perseveres nonetheless.

Rumblings of dissent threaten to disturb the custodians of the status quo, but in coming decades they will find that this genie will not be going back willingly into the bottle.

One of the tropes circulating in the culture wars at this time causes me to speak up against the already lame defence that we are 'born this way'. Let me clarify …

Yes, I choose!

In an ethics course at the Institute, we discuss what I feel is a pitifully weak rationale doing the rounds of the community, apparently in response to the conservative Christian accusation that we are not born gay, that we are simply immoral (even 'toevah'; in Hebrew, an 'abomination'); that we in fact *choose* to be this way. That seems to be the crux of the issue: either there is a genetic basis to variant sexual orientations, or we are morally damnable folk who have *chosen* perversity, wilfully making love against the natural order.

'It's Adam and Eve, not Adam and Steve!' they snarl for my edification, these only rudimentarily educated amateur theologians, casting back to a flat-footed, sketchy knowledge of the writings of displaced Israelites.

I detest the weak and plaintive rejoinder offered from our side of the battle lines: 'Do you think I would actually *choose* to be this way? That I would choose to be discriminated against, thrown in jail, have my livelihood threatened; that I would choose to be harassed by the police; even cast out from my family?' 'And so on. If it were a choice, why would I choose pain; etc., etc? Ergo, 'I *must* have been born this way.'

I find this a pusillanimous argument, too suggestive of a 'victim' mentality, and constructed entirely within the context of conventional binary assumptions. Whatever the real nature and aetiology of this 'condition' might be, then, how can I understand it, deal with it in any way, unless I choose to face the music and own it squarely first?

I can't leave it to the religious types, with their hostility scarcely concealed beneath their protestations of compassion. And of course, there are some who do the opposite of concealing their hostility; the Westboro Baptist Church in Kansas being a conspicuous purveyor of hate speech. Picketing funerals of gay people with shocking signs claiming that GOD HATES GAYS and citing verses from the Holy Bible.

Nor can I trust psychology – struggling itself to find respectability as a science – that has decreed that I suffer from a *pathological* condition, a failure along a 'normal' (or normatively defined) developmental pathway.

Self-respect is up to me.

More than that, I am forced to consider that 'coming out' is an *assertive* spiritual practice, as well as a political stance, because intuitively I know that my 'condition' cannot only be about sexuality.

So, using the Internet as my platform, I start to take up a contrarian position: Yes, I do CHOOSE to be 'gay', but in a way quite different, and with quite a different effect than what you might assume. Odious word, that 'gay' is almost as shallowly rooted as 'homosexual'! If anything, I prefer 'queer'. (But that's not a popular choice in these parts.)

I pose it as an existential choice. I claim that it is a very healing thing to do – as an existential being, starting my life afresh, this very moment – to OWN what I am; to embrace the complexity of my being, flush out all negative attitudes about myself, within me, and stake my claim to being whole, here, now; an equal member of the race. I claim the right to define my life on my own terms, without accepting the ready-made interpretations of the meaning of my life provided by hostile, or even kindly disposed, but nonetheless patronising discourses.

To stake that claim, of my own volition and in full possession of my faculties, is to radically *choose to be who I am*; to cherish my life and all the opportunities it brings as I discover them, afresh. For, out of that healing, new signs of growth in awareness and understanding, come.

Whatever is blocking the light shifts aside and I begin to understand myself better, from within and without.

And I notice that many people tend to accord respect towards people who have self-respect. Or, if they can't afford the minimum respect due to me as a citizen, with full and equal rights, let them slink away into the shadows of their own fears, repelled by the brightness of my radiant being.

That choice frees me, now, to parent myself and relinquish blaming others (parents, authority figures, churchmen and women, doctors, politicians, *et al.*) and really grow into the fullness of being, to *discover* for myself what I can become. Our parents did what they could (some more than others, to be sure), given the limitations of their understanding, in a great chain of intergenerational indoctrination. But their responsibility is over when I take on the responsibility for my own life. Choosing to be what I am, heals an inner divide, then. Also, instead of being the victim of some genetic quirk, it brings all my power back to me, in the present. If there are feelings that this kind of affirmation brings up that don't sit easily alongside such confidence, it's obvious where the healing needs to take place: I need to do some work on myself to heal the deep-seated sense of shame that inevitably gets dislodged, and bridge the separation of self from self, produced by *internalised* homophobia. Maybe then a better understanding of how to be what I am will emerge from the rubble.

All around me people are dying of AIDS. Even now that we know how the HIV virus can be transmitted, people are still becoming infected, fully aware that they might be taking on a death sentence. What is this will to self-destruction? Have we bought into the construction being promulgated by the radio talk-show crusader Dr. Laura Schlessinger, that we are 'biological errors' (a position that she later denies taking); that by not breeding, we are not supposed to actually even *be* here?

The greater challenge I see now is to recognise my queer nature as a *gift*. To free myself to explore that potential beyond the strictures of fear. Furthermore, I have the opportunity to honour the gift and encourage a supportive environment to nurture my special nature and discover what has lain undeveloped, hidden away by the force of unquestioned, prevailing toxic teachings. Why 'criminal', 'diseased outsider', 'pervert', 'abomination'? We have been subjected to systematic emotional manipulation, even disguised as the love of concerned families; even the 'love' of big Father God himself.

Meanwhile, these authorities would cheat us from realising our potential, decontaminated of their ignorance. For my generation, and those that will follow, that will no longer be good enough!

The spectre of AIDS brings these issues into high relief. A perhaps unexpected side effect is the upswell of compassionate service from lesbian women towards young men stricken by the deadly virus, and a healing of a division within the community between the two wings of 'queer'. And scholarly papers are even being written about a nascent turn towards spirituality.

In quite pragmatic, everyday terms, I have found that such an approach works better than wasting my energy boxing shadows. They have created straw men to fight, but I really am not made of straw.

Let me just take a deep breath, feel all that freely available energy flowing unrestricted into my being; let it pop open those constricted places in my heart and dance me joyously through this zone in which I find myself. I call upon all the enlightened beings on every plane to protect and guide me, to fill me with the energy to fulfil my life's purpose in the most productive way possible, to become all that I can be.

When I was travelling as a meditation instructor on behalf of my Teacher, I remember meeting a man during one of my visits to Taiwan. A woman brought her husband along to one of the meetings, hoping that he would benefit from the teachings. The poor man had been disfigured facially in an industrial accident, and his face was so badly scarred it was only possible to make out the basic features through the twisted, ugly scarring. Needless to say, he was depressed and sad and gloomy. I explained to him that what we were teaching was a way to look within, using ancient meditation practices, and re-discover our lives from the essential core of being.

I don't want to dismiss this poor man's suffering. The face he was presenting to the world was gruesome to behold, and I could feel that he wanted to shrink away in shame, but I knew that to find the inner peace and joy could transform his experience of being in the world. While his face remained 'ugly', even repulsive, to a casual observer, he could recover his self-respect and re-build a life not dictated by what had happened to his body. I hoped that by persevering in the inwardly focused practices of meditation he could slowly repair his sense of self from within.

This might sound glib, presented in just a few words, but I knew from personal experience how attending the meetings and learning to listen from the heart to the testimonies shared from the heart, was the beginning of a shift in feeling that could take you all the way home.

That 'you are not your body, you are not your mind, you are something lying deep behind', to paraphrase a favourite song often shared in such gatherings.

In the same way, if your sense of identity has been twisted and distorted by toxic versions of what is given to you by the foolish indoctrinations of institutionalised religion and jejune psychologists, it is simply not necessary to internalise that version of identity. You can throw off that mask and liberate yourself. Those constructions are not set in stone.

It's up to me to cast aside fear and embrace a fuller vision of humanity. If I haven't done so in my own life, I can't expect my opponents to recognise something of worth in me. There is no room in my heart for their visions of misery.

So, if you wish to join me in celebration, you are welcome; but if you wish to walk through a Valley of Tears, let that be your own choice. And no, I don't have to live on the margins of society. Nor do I have to storm its barricades. Nor will I accept being merely tolerated; I don't want to fit in. Nor do I want to walk around with a gigantic chip on my shoulder, accusing individuals – as representatives of an ethic they may not even understand – of being agents of repression.

The forms of religion here in late 20th century USA have taken upon themselves as their primary duty the policing of conventional gender boundaries. It's a cosy conspiracy and it has enlisted powerful tools of persuasion to reinforce its hold over our minds and our lives: Religion, psychological Medicine, Madison Avenue, the Military, the news Media, Capitalism itself; all participate in the repression!

I don't need to smash that system to be free. Let them have it. Let them enjoy the fruits of their toxic, miserable lies. But I now reclaim my original *innocence* and, through a process of healing, arrive at a place where I can celebrate being and discovering just what I am, wholly.

But this is America and the culture wars are raging. I have to develop my own rationale to defend myself, here in the late 1990s, against the backdrop of a deadly virus and a conservative religious community. Their occasional, fatuous claims that one or other natural disaster is caused by the moral decline of gay folk simply fails to convince. A prominent preacher who has founded his own university, claims that a hurricane in Florida was caused by gay men dancing at Disneyworld in Orlando …

To me, their 'God' is a constructed effigy, made in their own image, their Jesus pitifully re-cast as an apologist for middle-class morality. Are they afraid of love, when love is the most powerful force in the universe? To my understanding they have established this anti-Christ of judgement and morality in its place. Jesus was a radical.

My Teacher has pointed me towards an inner resolution of fear and the fostering of true understanding, and since 1972, his coaching continues to support my efforts to dig for the personal resources I need to draw on to respond to the peculiar challenges life is bringing me.

My 'God' is intimately close to my being, sustaining my every breath; His/Her light is the life that gives me life. I will allow nothing to come between me and that power, I am equally blessed with its gifts and, thanks to three decades of meditation practice, under the guidance of my patient Teacher, I know the one original gift that makes all the rest possible. I draw my life from the one source, I drink from the well that waters all life; it is bubbling away within, and it slakes my thirst. It gives me life and inspires me. I am its expression in the world, an integral part of the creation, still evolving.

In me 'God' is knowing him/herself, enjoying his/her work. I am his/her agent, the giver and recipient of all gifts.

In a binary world of idiotic, strictly exclusive opposites, I am content to be the one who resolves duality. I am Androgyny: male and female in one original form. If you cannot embrace wholeness and would push away the parts of being that your improper indoctrination into the binary codes of this society have taught you to reject, then yes, for you I am your *Devil*, the projection of the darkness that you stuff down inside of you, to lurk in the shadows of your fear.

Until you begin to recognise me as yourself, you will continue to mistake my true spiritual identity, as an equal child of life, and you will not be free. Come and stand with me in the light of self-acceptance and know that deep within, where you may transcend the little ego self, you are one with God, and in that reality *we are all fundamentally the same.*

Spirituality and psychology must overlap, don't they? If I can stand up now, to be counted as a whole person, re-integrating those parts of my Self split off by fear-filled indoctrination, I do that on behalf of all. I am the wounded healer, and in my own healing I awaken that powerful archetype within. For me, that's a more potent force for me to work with than the blood of the martyr.

Meanwhile, aside from all the political responses to forces on all sides, I remember something my Teacher, Prem, has said, so simply: 'If you're looking at a map to tell you how to get to a place, the first thing you have to do is locate where you are on the map.' That's your starting point. So, here I am. QED. In persevering with a daily meditation practice, my ethical conscience is tweaked. Incidents from the day come up for review and an increasingly sensitive, intuitive feeling becomes the guide that shows me the quality of my actions when they are not considerate of the needs of others. No book of rules can arbitrate with the finesse required to assay my ethics.

I come across a discussion group on CompuServe where a group of faceless Christians are earnestly discussing the Biblical injunction that gays should be put to death (I believe the recommended method is by stoning; some righteous countries following the old codes still use this recommended method of punishment; others force us to jump from high buildings to our deaths; while others deploy less subtle adherents to beat us to death with their fists, their feet, their baseball bats, and so on).

Needless to say, I wade into that discussion without delay. Even for someone whose 'gaydar' is highly unreliable, I recognise some sister spirits among proponents in the group and I advise one of them, who has been sending me snide attacks, aside from the main discussion board, that even were he to wallpaper it with pages of sacred scripture, the closet would always be an unhealthy place.

I find it strange that toxic attitudes towards other human beings could be rationalised so thoroughly in the name of Christian morality, that bigotry should dress itself up as righteousness, of all things … but I suspect that may be its favourite disguise.

On the national edition of CBS Evening News, news anchor Connie Chung reports on the case of a man charged with murder. He accepted the invitation of a gay man to have sex … and then killed him. He claims that while he has indeed killed, he can be assured of going to 'Heaven' while his victim will be going to the other place; because he is a Christian and can confess and ask forgiveness, while the other bloke ... I'll spare you the rationale.

A controversy erupts in Colorado, where citizens succeed in getting an anti-gay ballot up for a state-wide vote. The case captures national attention. The coach of the college football team in Denver – they are national champions, and he has considerable status in his milieu – throws his weight behind the anti-gay campaign, but he is chastised by the University's president for using his position to push his barrow while standing at a lectern that displays the University's crest.

Among the letters to the editor of a Denver morning newspaper I notice that the pastor of a church has written in to affirm 'Biblical support' for the position of the football coach. I track down the address of the church and open up a correspondence with the reverend gentleman in charge. I ask him to explain the incident (recounted in John, chapter 8, verses 3-11 of the 'New Testament') where Jesus is asked about the punishment of a woman caught in adultery. (You might ask where the missing sinner male is situated in this narrative!)

According to the 'law of Moses', it's a righteous act to stone her, apparently, but Jesus sends her accusers slinking away with the rebuke that only 'he who is without sin should cast the first stone'.

In his reply to me, the minister points out that, even after the accusers depart, Jesus advises the woman to 'go and sin no more'. Check.

So I propose to him, if he wishes to take on the role of Jesus in deciding what is sin and who is a sinner, whether he is also prepared to step in, as Jesus did, to protect the 'sinner' from the 'righteous'. I ask whether I can now expect to hear of him using his pulpit to actually speak out against the proposed law and defend homosexuals from such righteous folk as the coach of the winning football team.

After demanding to know whom I represent, the reverend gentleman cuts off all further communication. Check mate.

Or is it stalemate?

If I hadn't recognised religion, especially as it is constituted in such a society, as the source of a great deal of wrong-headed and mean-spirited homophobia, perhaps you will make allowances for the fact that at this time I am expressing my most de-stabilising spiritual questioning, for it is a wise and compassionate teacher, ostensibly from an 'Eastern' tradition, who has the means to help me, and he has never placed thorns in my path to do with my sexuality. He says that 'when the sun shines, it shines for everybody' and I have always taken that to mean that, if there is such a thing as a 'deity' (a concept I can live quite easily without, while continuing the empirical practices which take me deeper and deeper into the mystery of being), it might be equally available, not just for 'good' people.

If I had taken on the guilt trips offered by religion as I have encountered it, I would certainly be dead. Do I need to spell out the ways? I am extremely fortunate that my Teacher and 'life coach' holds this vision of me as whole, and the healing that has come from my own experiences of that root self, sustained over many years of assiduous practice, has been the force that has shown me what it means to save a life, rather than lose it. And I am developing a certain strength, from within as he has worked to transform me from *vic*-tim to Victor.

Testing the limits

I go to Boston for one of those international convocations of scientists arranged by the AAAS (The American Association for the Advancement of Science), where science journalists are welcome. The producers of *Beyond 2000* accept that it might be useful, and they pay my way to attend. (The airfares don't cost them anything, as they accrue all the frequent flyer points from their crews on the road, so it's just a weekend in another city.)

It's winter and here on the East Coast, there's plenty of snow. People are bemused at the sight of me walking outdoors, when they are scurrying, intent to get inside and out of the cold. As an inhabitant of sunny Southern California I can indulge in such pleasures; the white blanketing of snow brings out a romantic side of me.

From my hotel, I walk briskly over to the convention centre to present myself for this year's instalment of Victor's continuing re-education program, ready to throw myself in the deep end of Science again. Let's see if there's anything I can grasp …

But outside, a few yards from the entrance to the Center, a long trestle table has been set up by some association of high school science teachers. I don't have to consult their pamphlets to know what they are proselytising, for their large banner reads:

TEACH GEOMETRY NOT FAGGOTRY IN THE SCHOOLS

Not quite the welcome I had in mind.

Their literature protests against the initiative in a school district in New York to introduce what they are calling a 'Rainbow Curriculum'. There has been some controversy about the district's attempts to acknowledge the real-world diversity in the population groups served by the schools and, apparently, resistance to the initiative is not restricted to conservative religious groups. *Heather Has Two Mommies* is a controversial text. Now here in Boston, this group of high school *science* teachers wants to strongly register their protest against such a development. Are they a part of a national campaign?

I try to strike up a discussion with the young man behind the table, but it is a very brief encounter.

'What are you teaching in the schools?' I ask him. 'It seems to me you are pushing stereotypical thinking.'

From his side, a truculent refusal to engage with me.

'You know, your sign is very offensive to me,' I say. 'It's hate speech. Will you please remove it?'

'No way, *faggot*!' he snarls, coming straight to the point. (This is a *science* teacher?)

A flush of anger rises through me. I grip the table firmly with both hands and heave it upside down. Pamphlets and books go flying across the icy sidewalk.

While the 'high school science teacher' is surprised and flustered by my assertiveness, I have little time to consider what my next move might be, as there's someone tapping on my shoulder.

I turn to face a hard, clenched fist smashing into my chin.

Ouch. The teacher has back-up. I also see from his eyes that my assailant is extremely pleased the situation has escalated to a climax that allows him to express his zeal so forthrightly. These Boston boys are inclined to be pugnacious.

Outnumbered, I retreat to the safer confines of the convention centre itself, where I complain to the security guard inside.

For the next few days the hinge of my aching jaw is a reminder that confrontation might not always be the best way to proceed with my 'enemies', but I am pleased to note that the science teachers' information table is nowhere in evidence for the rest of the conference.

My letter of complaint to the office of the Mayor of Boston fails to draw a response.

Coming out, spiritually

My close friend, a remarkably astute New Yorker named Susan Peters, refuses to accompany me to the annual festival of queer film which is held at the Director's Guild complex on Sunset Boulevard.

I have little time for the usual campy comedies, but there is a surprising range of international movies that just don't get released into US movie houses, let alone on television. And some of them feature storylines that include friendships between gay men and their girl friends.

But Susan digs her heels in. We have worked on shows together, and in many ways she has been a real ally, so I just don't understand her resistance on this.

'I wouldn't go to those any more than I would go along to a Black Power rally! If you want to identify as a minority, that's your problem, not mine' seems to be the basis of her objection, which throws me for a loop. She feels that you weaken your position if you bleat for special treatment. And I do understand that. She also feels uncomfortable about my studying at IGLE but puts up with it.

'And why the gay thing anyway? You meditate, don't you?' (Susan has even been along to hear a talk by my Teacher at an event in Pasadena.)

Jewish or not, Susan goes to an alternative church in West LA, popular with hipsters, which has a brilliant choir, comprised mostly of session musicians, rocking out for Jesus. The pastor, Reverend Michael, is affiliated with the 'Science of Mind' movement and he spins a good yarn in his sermons. The name of Jesus is still invoked here. While Susan gets off on the abundant Holy Roller energy, I prefer the quiet, inward focus of meditation.

Susan is an attentive and generous friend, and we share some odd forms of entertainment. For example, we like to watch beauty pageants on TV together. National or international, it makes no difference. On occasions when we're not viewing side by side in the same room, we'll do it by phone. We set up a competitive format where we try to pick the top ten contestants from the initial walk-down as the beauties are introduced one by one, but Susan cheats the system. Her top ten swells to twelve, fourteen, sixteen or more, but she still claims a win if anyone from her list makes the final; while I try to play by my self-imposed rules.

Nothing thrills her more than the time she gets invited to a be a judge on a pageant to select the winner of an international 'Mrs competition', for married women, and it's staged in Costa Rica (Susan is fluent in Spanish).

I don't think Susan has ever paid any attention to the proposition that there might be such a thing as a third gender. It's not a new idea. In South Sulawesi, among the Bugís people, there's a recognition of five gender types. (Sydney Jewish Psychotherapist Kim Gotlieb points out that there are *five* genders noted in the Talmud.)

I don't feel confronted by my friend's interrogation, but it's a fruitful encounter for me because, for the first time, I find myself saying: 'It's not just about sex.' Isn't it obvious that such activities are a normal variation of human sexual behaviour (and have been evident throughout history)? This is how I have come to understand it so far: When I agreed to come to this zone of human existence, I accepted that I would be part of a minority, a despised and marginalised minority, and it is part of my spiritual work – my *dharma*, if you like – to not only continue to work on my own 'salvation', if you will, but to help build a bridge back from the margins, for people who might feel shut out of the social contract, and with no pass into 'Heaven'.

I surprise myself. I have never articulated this position in the past. Later I will move to a further understanding that, as you are drawn out of a fixed sense of self through experience rather than belief, you might come into a deeper sense of reality in which rigid divisions are rendered invalid.

The original 'Los Angeles Gay Film Festival' soon becomes the 'Los Angeles Lesbian and Gay Film and Video Festival'; until it becomes almost impossible to spread the umbrella of inclusiveness in words and types of gender and sexuality. How many types of human are there? And does that make the society weaker, or stronger? Some 'gay' Americans refuse to allow 'Queer' as a signifier under any circumstances and that disagreement still bubbles on. Language can be weaponised. The festival of film and video eventually becomes, simply, OutFest, but at the time of writing, we are still trying to get it right with the unwieldy LGBTQIA+, which threatens to topple its overladen baggage. One day we must surely return to becoming and being accepted as 'humans'.

Meanwhile, it's IGLE that is helping me work through some basic issues ...

Two-spirit

If the conventional religion of my culture offers little helpful insight, and science is a battleground fraught with its own disagreements, I start to dig into the work of anthropologists who have uncovered evidence of how folk like me might have been treated in other cultures.

I take the chance to meet one of them when I go to a talk at IGLE, given by Walter Williams from the University of Southern California, who has researched the gender conventions among indigenous people in North America and further afield.

Dr Williams has done fieldwork among living representatives of the *berdache*, or 'two-spirit' tradition in Amerindian and other indigenous societies. (Later he will drop this particular colonial-era term, *berdache*, in favour of 'two-spirit'.) He has also researched early historical reports of contact between the explorers, traders and missionaries with these figures, who exhibited certain mixed gender attributes, often excelling in the skills and crafts of their so-called 'opposite' gender and usually including 'cross-dressing', with a mixture of clothing from across the apparent gender divide. Before colonial times, they were usually highly respected, even venerated, and often regarded as being 'spiritually gifted' in their own first-nation settings.

It's exciting for me to hear of these ancient traditions in other cultures, and I listen avidly. Years ago, when I was an undergraduate student in Perth, I studied a full year unit in anthropology. Now there is within me a growing understanding of the potential value of what is so often cast outside the boundaries; an inkling that – rather than being a cruel rejection, as painful as it can be – the violence of exclusion might be taken as a provocation to seek out more life-enhancing teachings to realise an enhanced fullness of being.

Williams explains the customs, social roles, and history of these figures, and traces the introduction of the European concepts of sin and subsequent intolerance towards sexual and gender diversity. It's not too much of a stretch to identify with them, as the boy who briefly loved to wear the yellow dress.

They were present among First Nations peoples right across North America, reaching further south into some parts of Central and South America and north across Canada, into Siberia, etc. Williams also traced similar traditions in Polynesian cultures.

Known by various names in different language groups – *winkte* in Lakota Sioux, *nadle* in Navajo, *he man he* among the Cheyennes, *mexoga* in Omaha, the Zuni *Ihamana*, etc., variously translated as 'not man, not woman', halfman-halfwoman, etc. These 'two spirit' people were recognised as early as in their childhood; welcomed into their tribes and regarded as being gifted as mediators between men and women, as well as between the world of Spirit and their human societies. They became powerful, even feared advisors. Those who honoured them benefited from their participation in the life of the tribe.

Such was the attitude before colonial times.

My curiosity was immediately piqued. From my earliest days I was warned against crossing the line, with all the coercive forces of social conditioning working to keep me on the right side of the divide. But I have been having fun playing at de-stabilising the binary with my costume play at Halloween, and now I am being nudged to look more deeply into the roots of that 'play'.

The Abrahamic traditions spread across the world as colonising projects, each reckoning that there is a divinely ordained imperative operating within their systems, and powerful sanctions deriving from those traditions are still conspicuously expressed today. But here I am being presented with evidence from other ancient cultures, where the metaphysical and religious framing allowed, respected and *valued* conspicuous variants to the binary arrangement.

Looking for examples among the fragmented and scattered descendants of various groups, Williams approached his informants as an 'out, gay' anthropologist, earning their trust to such a degree whereby, in some situations, he was introduced to living exponents of the tradition who had been otherwise hidden, denied or suppressed, post-colonisation.

Because it is such a powerful force in the world today, the Western Judaeo-Christian tradition is often accepted as the arbiter of 'natural behavior' of humans. If Europeans and their descendant nations of North America accept something as normal, then anything different is seen as abnormal. Such a view ignores the great diversity of human existence. [p.61]

In preparing his research, Williams contacted surviving members of this group and retrieved important information about a tradition that had been all but extirpated since the crushing advent of the missionaries. Typically, fixating on sexual behaviour and elements of cross-dressing, enabled the colonists to overlook the honoured role these people played in their traditional cultures. Unable to see outside the prism of their own preconceived notions, they completely overlooked the gifts the 'two spirit' people gave back to their communities.

Anglo American society and family structure gives only a grudging tolerance to the non-masculine male, at best, while in American Indian cultures, to use the words of a Lakota, 'If a *winkte* is in a family, that family would feel fortunate.' [p.62]

As Williams describes the experience of these honoured members of the tribe, in our IGLE classroom in the West Hollywood fire station, I feel a palpable wave of energy pass through the group that literally gives me goosebumps. To hear about a society in which one's differently ordered nature would be recognized, respected, and highly valued is exciting in a way I think any class of 'outsiders' could relate to. I need to know how this welcoming affects the development of their consciousness, when it is not twisted by shaming? I can't become an indigenous American; I have to find out how it might develop in my own very particular circumstances.

Imagine growing up 'bent' in a society that *didn't* regard you as somehow spoiled, broken, even *pathological*. How would children turn out in modern Western societies if they were allowed to explore the natural expression of their innate natures with honour and respect, instead of shame?

The *berdache* is not expected to suppress his tendency for feminine behaviour. Neither does he internalize a low self-image. He thus avoids the tendency of those considered deviant in Western culture to engage in self-destructive behavior. Berdaches who value their traditions do not tend to be alcoholic or suicidal, even in tribes where such problems are common. They are too valued by their families ... A Crow traditionalist says, 'We don't waste people, the way white society does. Every person has their gift.' [p. 57]

For an alienated minority today, the wisdom of that inclusiveness is not only of anthropological interest, to me it presents a tantalising vision of what could have been in my own society. Together we dream of living in a world where we would neither be stigmatised nor marginalised, but welcomed as useful, with special strengths and talents; not better than other people but gifted with different talents.

So, as I said to Susan, it's not just about sex. That's a very crude tool to identify oneself by; it simply doesn't give room to find out what else might be expressed. In the wider frame, any society that shuts out some of its most creative energies by damning non-conformists loses the contribution of its total membership and eschews some of the strength that diversity can bring.

Most interesting, Williams reports that one of his informants, a Hawaiian *mahu*, has said to him:

On the mainland [referring to the United States] the religion doesn't allow a culture of acceptance. Gays have liberated themselves sexually, but they have not yet learned their place in a spiritual sense. [p. 258]

I get an inkling, then, that there is work to be done in more than just the legal and the political spheres, even as they are providing their own opportunities.

I come across several others who try to bridge the gap between the way modern Western societies view identities beyond the two-dimensional model. In their re-examination of shamanistic practices, Jenny Blain and Robert Wallis suggest:

> It may be that men whose sexuality is ambiguous, or who are marginalised because of sexuality, are in a position where they must attend to levels of meaning that escape from or that are not obvious to those privileged by dominant discourses of gender [p. 399].

In his study of the 'gynemimetic' shaman, William Dragoin writes of the 'associated talents' of sexual inversion, which include ecstatic trance, and he proposes that:

> contrary to the idea of illness or defect ... such an individual might better be considered talented or gifted, with a readiness to learn to enter a trance state or a native ability to readily alter ordinary states of consciousness, and in so doing become the ecstatic visionary ... to become the shaman for one's people. [p. 227].

Dragoin concludes that such individuals have been a part of non-literate societies for millennia.

The memory of my early experiment as a three-year old, with my mother's yellow dress, starts to stir in response. And I have since come to understand those events in an entirely new way. Being so rudely disappointed by the brutalising indoctrination into masculine codes and shutting off respect for other talents, I had to hide my interests in that direction. What that disappointment could have become – attempting to change my gender by intervening with crude surgical and hormonal adjustments to locate the 'missing' feminine – I understand now, was an atavistic yearning for the state of un-differentiated unity from which I had not yet evolved. I wasn't trying to be female! The state of unity was first, with gender a secondary development, and sexuality a distant third. Plenty of opportunities for confusion along that developmental pathway!

The famous anthropologist Ruth Benedict, who taught Margaret Mead, also considered the significance of the North American 'berdache', observing that a culture may 'value and make socially available even highly unstable human types' [Benedict, 233]. If such a culture chooses to treat the 'peculiarities' of these 'types' as valued variants of human behaviour, Benedict finds that the individuals in question might 'rise to the occasion' and perform useful social roles without reference to the 'usual ideas' of the types that can function in our society. Further, she points out, those who 'function inadequately' in any society are not those with 'abnormal' traits, *per se*, but may well be those 'whose responses have received no support' from the institutions of their culture; those whose 'native responses' were not reaffirmed by society.

I begin to understand that the constructions produced within the social and political contexts of one's time are ideologically charged and quite particular artefacts of culture, politically and epistemologically constructed at any point in history. They are not universal laws of a putative 'human nature'.

Perhaps to recover from the state of amnesia concerning my true role I will have to recuperate parts of my queer nature lost to me, heretofore, by my society's homophobic conditioning. And it reinforces my doubts about how a misguided religious culture that has itself run off the rails, might see its main role as the policing of gender boundaries in these 'godless' times! By insisting on their warped and limited imaginary, they are cheating me of a fullness of being. When will I realise: self-respect is up to me?

Stepping outside of the Abrahamic traditions to learn of other possibilities of meaning and knowing, constructed with different values by other cultures, helps me to destabilise the presumed authority of forms of knowledge that might be politically powerful now. Those approved, culturally sanctioned ways of knowing are arranged to switch off certain neural pathways or potentials as prohibited, no-go zones.

'Coming out' in a hostile setting (family and socially) requires courage, but I feel that 'coming *in*' might well be a *spiritual* process. For I use the term 'spirituality' as a deep and sincere inquiry into the mystery of being. Rather than throwing off the shadow of shame and being satisfied with settling there, (preferably with a loving partner, a white picket fence and a pair of dogs) just might not be the end of the story.

This growing awareness doesn't land fully formed, all at once, and I read work by Will Roscoe and Judy Grahn and others. And I will pick up on this train of thinking again some decades later, when I come across fascinating testimony in the form of an autobiography named: *Of Water and the Spirit* by a modern-day shaman from Burkina Fasso), named Malidoma Somé.

When I was growing up, religion was part of a sociological system of inclusion and exclusion, gathering some within, and others outside the fold. Apparently, in this set of narratives, 'God' is the biggest homophobe, and this particular construction of divinity betrays its myopic human authorship. I find myself saying that the ideas of 'God' at any point in time and space says more about the notions of the culture that produces the 'God' than it says about the nature of that Figure.

These are the ideas that are helping me understand a new way of being otherwise shut down by shaming.

But I can now feel how fortunate I am. The ground for effecting this shift in my thinking has been thoroughly prepared, for the amnesia induced by my initiation into binary gender codes has been alleviated by years of sustained meditation practice, re-introducing the numinous aspects of being into conscious awareness and carrying me back into the deep awareness of the root of being itself, upon which all the rest depends.

The 'Ground of Being' it will be called; a state I was innocently accessing in my play with the yellow dress, aged around three, before the emergence of dominant local gender rules. And, later when I am writing my book about Christopher Isherwood, I read Andrew Harvey, who had written translations of some of the poems of the ecstatic Persian sage known simply as Rumi, in the West, one of which reads:

Once you have tied yourself to selflessness,
you will be delivered from selfhood
and released from the snares of a hundred ties …

The refrain that tags each verse of the poem runs: 'so come, return to the root of the root of your own self'. [Harvey. 51].

Implicit in the mystic's call is the teaching that the missing 'root' of connectedness won't be found outside the self; nor is it found *as* the self. Rumi is pointing even deeper than the self, then, suggesting that 'self' is rooted within the Divine, sine qua non; that the connection is the very root of being. And it must be known as a felt experience, by direct contact; not through doctrines, rituals and belief, but deep within the soul awareness, as conscious lived experience.

As Thomas Merton writes of the Chinese sage with whom he found so much in common: 'Chuang Tzu is not concerned with words and formulas about reality, but with the direct existential grasp of reality in itself. Such a grasp is necessarily obscure and does not lend itself to abstract analysis.' [Merton. p. xvi]

When I try to invoke this state, some of my well-educated friends feel I am attacking Reason itself. They are grateful that the superstitions of religion as they have experienced it, have been cast off. They are suspicious when I suggest that Reason is a limited, if useful, operation of mind, and it's certainly valid, on its own terms; but as a tool for exploring the field of consciousness itself, it's rather limited.

Some meditation practices should be respected as empirical research, not operating from belief, which is a different operation of mind.

Pushing further, I would now respectfully propose that if we queer folk want to centre our own self-narratives strictly around the genital expression of sexuality, we are at risk of losing the fullest apprehension of our *faerie* potential which, from my experience, can be reclaimed without in any way repudiating our sexuality. 'Faerie men have to dream their own mythologies,' says my friend Peter Savastano, from Princeton. We must research new/old ways of being in our own bodies, here and now, in this world.

Much later, at a conference of Asian and Pacific scholars in Sydney I will feel a similar frisson when a professor from southern India describes the androgynous Hindu deity Ardharanisvara, a Siva/Sakti representation that blends male and female elements in a representation of divinity. A third gender was not an alien possibility in traditional Indic culture.

City of (lost) angels (i)

My studio apartment is at ground floor level on Hawthorn Avenue, one block south of Hollywood and two blocks north of Sunset Boulevard.

One Saturday night I come home late from a day trip out to visit old friends Mal & Jayne, who live and work way out in the Valley, near Thousand Oaks where Mal works in video production. I decline their offer to stay overnight and have driven all the way back to Hollywood to sleep in my own bed. Around 2 am, I wake up to some loud altercation on the street outside.

Urgent voices, raised in desperation ... a loud gunshot ... then dead silence.

I'm almost accustomed to the sound of automatic gunfire, even just a few blocks away, and LAPD helicopters sometimes hover overhead, low enough that the air thuds with the turning of their rotor blades, their searchlights flashing through my blinds. I must be living on the edge of a crime zone, but incidents are so commonplace that I seldom find news reports of particular incidents the next day.

Tonight, though, is different. This is very close. The altercation climaxed to a quick crescendo, and that gunshot was like a (very) full stop, that left the atmosphere extraordinarily quiet.

I creep over to my balcony's sliding door to peer out across my balcony. In the streetlight I see a figure in a nondescript overcoat lying flat out on the sidewalk in front of the neighbouring apartment complex. A second person is sitting slumped on a low brick wall.

The police arrive and arrest the second man and confiscate his handgun. Next morning, my landlord fills in the details. Drug deals are pretty common around these parts and the shadows formed by the overhanging balconies of the apartment block next door are a favourite spot for individuals to partake of their newly acquired drugs. The guy with the gun was the landlord next door. He often comes out to eject these dark figures from the property that he manages, and he has become heartily sick of the disturbance, especially as this usually happens after midnight. The guy he shot was a young drifter from Oregon. The police find drug paraphernalia in the pockets of his coat.

The hullabaloo that woke me up was the sound of the dead guy begging for his life. The police confiscate the manager's gun and release him the next day.

A young policewoman I know tells me of a vigilante apartment manager over in Silverlake who was getting increasingly frustrated with the number of break-ins to his car. He rigged up an alarm which would alert him up in his apartment, so he could descend on the unsuspecting burglar, and shoot him in the head. He's done it more than once.

There's an uneasy feeling circulating that these vigilantes are helping to 'clean up the neighbourhood'. Druggies are seldom mourned. I am on notice that the 'dark' side of the world can come up so close. I have to be mindful to keep my balance and not allow my sense of safety to be swamped by darkness.

Meetings with remarkable women (i)

I sign up for a series of talks convened by a psychologist in West Hollywood, Dr. Terry Oleson: 'Carl Jung and Gay Affirmative Psychology'. It's the early 1990s and Terry is presenting an alternative worldview that backs away from the standard psychiatric view that constructs any form of sexual expression falling outside the conventional norm as a distortion. Instead, a new generation of psychologists is developing a psychology that retrieves a positive, accepting view of this aspect of human sexual behaviour.

Terry's group will meet on Sunday nights and I'm glad of an opportunity to meet and talk that isn't centred on the bar scene. He runs it more like a seminar than a therapy group, and he starts each session with succinct presentations of one or other aspect of a Jungian approach to personal growth, with free-form discussions following. As I've never been able to afford formal 'therapy', I set the intention that I should learn something important to my growth.

I present myself with an open mind, eager to learn something personally useful. And it won't be the last time that Dr. Jung opens up my understanding of human potential beyond the teachings of Sigmund Freud and his cronies.

Oleson is the director of the Claremont Graduate University's Institute for Psychology, which grants professional accreditation to people setting up as psychologists after completing their degrees, and he really knows his stuff. He opens with the theory of the archetypes, the dynamics of regression and progression, and the process of individuation into a model of an integrated personality.

Terry's presentation of the Jungian model (like Robert Hopcke's in northern California) holds out the tantalising possibility that to be homosexual might not be pathological, that even without the label, perhaps each man could grow into fully realised individuation of selfhood without having to apologise for his special, allegedly 'deviant' nature.

Naturally, there's a lot of discussion of the male's relationship to the internal *anima* archetype. For Jung, the 'anima' represents the man's inner 'feminine', and Terry focuses the first meeting on that, presenting it like the theme of a symphony that will play out in unexpected and sometimes dramatic ways for me over the ensuing weeks.

I am forced to recognise that, even with my strongly pronounced 'feminine' side – the gentleness that had given my father so much angst and led me to believe that I wasn't a 'real' man – I might have been blocking the really comfortable accommodation of the female energy with my everyday identity. (Later I realise that it may have been blocking a comfortable accommodation of 'male energy' with my everyday identity, too.)

It's not surprising that a gay man might have an uncomfortable relationship with his feminine side. After all, it may have been stigmatised in the brutal role-modelling available during his early life. What happens to the anima when she is not acknowledged? Does the wise High Priestess turn into a bitter witch, and what's wrong with witches, anyway? Does a distorted relationship with the inner feminine produce the bitchy queen?

You think it wouldn't be such a stretch for a gay man to respect the feminine. Most of my best friends are women after all. Haven't I always respected women? I could be the very exemplar of the sensitive new age guy! This is all a bit of a shock to consider.

Beginning to play with this notion of the feminine anima side in men takes place in the week before Halloween, traditionally a time when all the shadows come out to play, and Terry draws out the archetypes of the *witch* and the *crone*. A week later, the next session will coincide with the night of Halloween itself and he invites us to come in costume if we wish, before going on to the celebrations on the Boulevard in Boystown after the seminar.

I enter into the spirit of play, whipping up a costume from two second-hand stores in Pasadena and closer to home, a yard sale in West Hollywood. A character emerges who becomes 'the wicked witch of androgyny'. Or, as I introduce the old dame, my 'Aunt Regina', careful to explain the pun to anyone who will listen. She will sing songs from a private repertoire to entertain her adoring boys.

A long black dress in stretch fabric, which gives room to my middle-age girth. A black reefer jacket – Charles Jourdan; very suave don't you know – which I wear over a lacy black blouse, blending male and female items of attire. A close-fitting black velvet hat, with a lace veil drooping across the face as a 'fascinator'. I slather on some blue eye shadow, mascara and eyeliner and darken my greying moustache with an eyebrow pencil.

This is my first drag outing since the days with the yellow dress, forty-five years ago, and I feel a new energy flowing through me in this experimental gender play.

Aunt Regina's appearance throws the seminar into an uproar. She explains to Terry and the guys that if they are looking for her nephew Victor, *he's* at home in the closet, where he keeps *her* locked up all the days of the year, and she is determined to enjoy herself on her one night out. She entertains them with an old revue song about a pansy growing in the garden and later that night on the Boulevard she gets tipsy and misbehaves. Before she puts her costume away she makes her nephew promise to let her out again, same time next year.

But the trans-formational energies have not had their way with me yet ... As I invite the archetypes to engage playfully with my conscious life, I have no inkling of just how the dominoes will fall in subsequent months.

A week or so later, I'm walking back towards my parked car after another futile visit to the disco, when a mound of rags lurches into view to my left.

'Hey...!'

My head swings around ... It's not a mound of rags at all but a human form, huddled on some steps, which gathers itself together and rises up to blurt out:

'I WANTS MY HUG!' Emphatically. Not one to be denied.

A moment's hesitation. She's female. African American. She's LARGE. She's living on the street. What does she want? Does she smell?

But something ventured, a trusting step, and I am engulfed by this mound of woman, who is hugging me unreservedly and whispering in my ear. Suddenly too close. But I let go a little more and hug her back. She whoops and grinds her pelvis against me. I stiffen up, predictably resisting the embrace. I want to leave, but she clutches at my arm and, risking a little more, I let her drag me over to the stoop.

Now she has her audience captive but she takes her time, smoking and drinking, and she spins me a tedious yarn. Is this going to go on forever? She shows me her drawings and before long she's demanding to know why they don't play Billie Holliday on the radio.

I protest. 'They *do* play Billie Holliday. Besides, I even have recordings of her music.'

'Naw,' she insists, 'they won't play her music because she was into DRUGS, that's why ... She was a junkie! I'm not into drugs,' she chortles. '*This* is MY drug' (as she raises her brown paper bag).

Prissy Victor knows that it's against the law to consume alcohol in public here in California.

'Mah drug ... is ... alcohol!'

Huddled together on the steps, not entirely impervious to the curious stares of the passersby, I wonder what on earth I'm doing here. I give in and go along with the ride.

I chirp on: 'Now this Billie Holliday, she was a powerful woman. In most towns they treated her really poorly, making her stay in different hotels from the white musos. But she was so powerful that through her art she made them all listen to her when she sang, didn't she? White people, black people; men and women ....'

She ignores my fatuous remarks. 'I'm gonna sing ... *Billie Holliday.*'

She wants to sing for me now, this drunken pile of rags who lives on the street? I want to leave, but something insists on a different response from me. Is it just the power of her will?

I risk letting go a little more.

Slowly, maddeningly, she smokes another cigarette, testing me, pushing at me with her words, sussing out where I'm at. I'm ready to say something about the repercussions caused by Miss Holliday's singing 'Strange Fruit' ...

'Come here!' She is ready at last.

She commandeers my head in the crook of her arm, so I can't move (she's a BIG mother!). Holding my head still, not cradled but secured so that my ear is pressed up to her mouth, she starts to croon into it, sweetly, intimately, like it's a microphone in a basement bar somewhere in Harlem. And lets her voice curl out from its dark hiding place to spin her song of woe …

Willow, weep for me; willow, weep for me, each syllable unfurling from deep within her.

OMG! She has an amazing voice and she sings with selfless abandon. Somehow, the alcoholism has beaten down her ego and the song itself has trained her voice as its perfect instrument. She sings it better than Billie Holliday. And it's a private performance, just for one.

Sonorous phrases wring out the secret drops of a woman's suffering:

Listen to my plea… The voice of Woman, wailing through the ages, encoded within these notes, mysteriously imprinted in this marriage of lyrics and music, now revealed via this dark priestess of the Shadow, Her perfect channel, chanting out the phrasing that matches perfectly the contours of her sorrow-drenched heart.

Her song rolls into me like waves from the deepest oceans and breaking, dark seas, on the shores of my heart.

Gone my lover's dream …
Lovely summer's dream
Gone and left me here …
To weep my tears into the stream

Sitting on a doorstep on the dirty sidewalk where hustlers troll for trade, I disappear. Unhinged from the ordinary, my mind is bobbing on a sea of joy. I am glad that I have risked this, giving in to each little tug away from safety and comfort, letting myself be yanked from my perch, and now, with so little warning, to be taken into a deep, dark embrace that totally engulfs me.

Willow, weep for me; willow, hear my plea …

Our eyes are closed. Her self-consciousness obliterated, her heart is free to let it roll out in all its fullest aspiration. The voice is like crushed velvet and the notes of the song ring through all the resonators a singer's body is capable of sounding.

I am her captive and I am free. I am flying through a deep, dark universe and Woman sings her blood's song just for me. She flows through my being with ease, from verse to chorus to verse to chorus.

Leave my heart a-breaking
And making a moan
Murmur to the night
To hide the starry light
So none will find me sighing
And crying all alone

After infinity in an hour, she finally lets me loose.

She wants money now (I felt it coming). I pull out some dollars from one pocket and she intuits that I have more. We haggle good-naturedly and she wants me to stay. I feel a law of diminishing returns threatening to dissipate my newfound intoxication and I wriggle to free myself gently from her clutches, surrendering my remaining cash to her importuning. She gives me a photocopy of a picture from a book: It's 'Lady'. Billy Holliday. Lady sings the blues.

I stagger off, releasing myself into the night to privately quaff the profound space broken clear inside my heart, breathing easily into the resonant silence revealed here again, by such an unexpected agent, at such an unexpected point in time, in Boys' Town, West Hollywood.

What is outside is finite; the infinite is connected to from within, and there, we meet. At one level, an alcoholic jazz singer. At one level, broken, but with a pure heart. At the same time a channel for a transmission from the Mother of All Sorrows.

I realise that 'Los Angeles' is a contraction of an earlier name: La Ciudad de la Reina de los Angeles. The City of the Queen of the Angels. And She has blessed me.

Amidst these spontaneous and unexpected exercises in re-awakening the Archetypal Feminine, I hear that a teacher I've heard about – Mother Meera, an incarnation of the Divine Mother, they say – has come out of India and has been living in Germany. The well-known British author and gay mystic Andrew Harvey has, in a sense, 'discovered' her and he interprets her silent teaching to the West.

The word is that the Mother will be coming to Los Angeles, and she could be giving *darshan*. I know a little of what that might entail from blessed experiences with my own guru, but this? I'm intrigued, but cautious. Would this be disrespectful?

My friend Ruth Strassberg, who always knows the right people, proposes that it might be possible to meet with the Mother, in person.

I still go to hear from my Teacher Prem several times a year. In fact, on the exact date of my 25th anniversary of being initiated into the practice, he coincidentally announces a one-day review of the practice to be held in Denver and I take the day off work to be there. But Prem doesn't formally give 'darshan' in the US – perhaps it seems inappropriate in this Western cultural setting – and I miss the intimacy of that close encounter, as brief as it usually is. These days I only see him on a stage, from a distance, although I'll take what I can get. I feel a little concerned that I ought not be evincing interest in another teacher when I already adhere to my own; and I have a rich and continuing history with him.

Nonetheless, a few days later when I hear that the plans for the Mother's visit have been dropped, I do feel a twinge of disappointment. I don't want to change vehicles, mid-journey; I'm just curious.

That very same night, while asleep, in a dream state I find myself lifted up into a profound embrace by a supremely loving energy that fills my heart so generously that, after drenching me thoroughly, it overflows, streaming out to join the universe of love.

It feels just like the time in the tent at the big festival in the orange grove in Kissimmee, when I virtually dissolved into ecstasy. Inside, outside, released into each other's arms. Tonight, I let myself go completely into that sweet and tender force and I know that I am deeply and completely loved by a force that totally obliterates all sense of separation. I know that at some level *I am* Love itself. Ultimately, there is no 'self' *other* than love. All other framings are temporary, delusional.

Gradually, the power of the experience collects and forms into a face; a woman's face, looking down into mine with the deepest, darkest eyes, and I know the infinite form of the Divine is gazing into my heart with calm compassion and total, unconditional acceptance. Stranger still, those eyes are the same eyes I have lost myself in before, when I have been with my Teacher, Prem, whose very name means love.

I feel tinier than a speck of dust and at the same time I know that I am incredibly fortunate to have this blessing flow into me, leaving me profoundly gladdened. When the face leaves, I find that I am covered in a thick layer of white ash – itself a symbolic blessing, apparently – leaving me with no room for doubt that God as Mother loves me, and that the feeling is mutual.

Is this only a dream?

While travelling as an instructor in Asia I was drawn to the figure of Kuan Yin, also known as Kannon in Japan. Some say that she is a version of the compassionate Boddhisattva, Avalokiteshvara (*Chenrezig* in Tibetan). Sometimes known as the 'Goddess of Mercy', in this form She represents the compassionate side of the Buddha, a representation that gradually split off as a separate entity in folk religion, maybe similar to the emergence of the Virgin Mary in Catholicism, perhaps.

If the Buddha is sometimes seen as a little austere – insisting that you meditate your way to salvation, in effect 'saving' yourself by your own diligence – a deep human need has projected this intercessionary figure into the pantheon.

I saw her quite unexpectedly during an introductory psychic training session run by Fran Napier in Melbourne some years ago. I had no idea what was going on, but I did as I was gently directed by dear Fran. With my eyes closed, and the inner space cleared by meditation, *She* suddenly appeared to my inner gaze. At first, far off and then approaching rapidly, flying through the inner sky, robes fluttering in the wind, until She flew right into my heart, leaving me in a state of deeply resolved, unspeakable peace.

Now, within days of the dream of the Mother, the same friend Ruth who told me of the possible visit of the Indian guru, tells me that a statue of Kuan Yin that she has been minding has been slightly damaged in an earth tremor. For some reason, neither Ruth nor the woman for whom she is minding it, want the figure back in their houses and, as I have admired it in the past, she asks if I would mind taking care of it for a while.

I accept in a state of wonder, unable to explain to Ruth about the synchronicity of it all. More than mere coincidence ...

Instead of sitting with both legs drawn up into formal meditation pose, in this figuration She has one leg up, and the other hangs down into the world below. This is why they pray to her in the East. She is the one who hears the cries of the world, like Avalokiteshvara or Chenrezig to the Tibetan Buddhists. And now She sits in my small apartment, calmly radiating Her compassionate wisdom nature. A physical embodiment of a mysterious energy that has been gently insisting on my attention all these weeks.

Whenever I witness her serenity I feel deeply calmed. My Tonkinese cat, Princess Plum Blossom, also loves to hang with her.

A little work with the archetypes, and all this energy has come bursting into my life! Even in my curiosity I could not have guessed at the palpable power dwelling among the deeper recesses of the psyche. It seems that I'm dealing with real forces here! If this is 'play', I could say it is the Divine Mother's play, or my guru's *leela*, playing with my tightly-wound head. Not a distant God figure, modelled along stern patriarchal lines; a powerful Goddess, of equal power, who is always ready to engage with Her devotees.

I remember a wildflower that used to grow near my childhood home in West Australia. As kids we called it the 'trigger plant' (genus *stylidium*, family *Stylidiaceae*). As the petals open, the little pistil is revealed, all curled up inside. When a bee comes along and lands on the petal, its weight is just enough to 'trigger' the pistil to spring open and dust the bee with pollen.

Even here in Hollywood, residing and working in the deepest bowels of delusion, reality comes bursting through to dust me with sacred magic, and I know that my little life is intimately interconnected within the matrix of all being.

A year later, when Halloween comes around again, I create the character of the dead bride that I describe elsewhere in this memoir, acting out the imagery of the *anima*, denied. Recalling the profound cosmic humour operating in this zone, I complete the characterisation by singing the old music hall song:

There was I, waiting at the church
Waiting at the church, waiting at the church
When I found he'd left me in the lurch
Lor', how it did upset me

I'm starting to wonder to what degree gender itself is a 'performance' of one kind or another and I suspect that a male who will not receive the wisdom offered by his inner 'opposite' will never win in the deadly power games of gender. 'Straight' men seem so lopsided, especially if dominated by a toxic form of the masculinity they so doggedly cultivate.

A year after that one struts her stuff I finally lock on to the best character of all for Halloween – the traditional celebration that invites the spirits of what have been denied to come out to play. With the help of a very creative girlfriend who makes Halloween outfits for her children, I work up a costume for Queen Victoria from a photo taken from her later, stout period. I am becoming Victor/Victoria! I use a cushion to tie over my backside to fill out her bustle and go to great pains to collect the right accessories. With an overstuffed, padded bosom and the generous rear end, she sails down the Boulevard like a large battleship.

To a TV news crew collecting video for the eleven o'clock news, Her Royal Majesty offers this soundbite:

'In my day, there was only one Queen, and *We* ruled an entire Empire. Nowadays, there are so many little queens running around! We are not amused!'

When she collects first prize for best costume in Trunks, the sports bar on the Boulevard that is ruled over by Richard Sattler, the doyenne and honorary guardian of the venue, I am glad to accept the cash, for the accessories alone have cost more than the prize money. Richard, as presiding queen, hands over the prize, but not the microphone, not at all happy to surrender the mic to this mere also-ran. My carefully rehearsed acceptance speech must be saved exclusively for the KNBC news crew.

So, it was about more than becoming a drag queen or trying to become a woman; it was the celebration of a wholeness that takes cognizance of a dimension beyond the physical, the social, and the political. I notice that some gay men, while prepared to dress up in drag for fun, often want to assert an almost hyper-masculine image of their identity. As 'drag queens', some will often sport bushy moustaches, and their buff pectoral muscles burst through their costumes. 'Gender fuck' – reversing the binary gender codes – becomes comedic.

If 'society' has been prepared to grudgingly allow our existence as second-class women, in coming out, are these 'gay' men asserting a fully rounded personality that incorporates both feminine and masculine qualities, with the bitter separation healed? Or is it just party, party, party on ...?

My sense of being at home in my own self has not come from gay liberation, it has come from the sustained discipline of the inwardly focused meditation practices and the ongoing relationship with my Teacher, a connection that will continue through several more changes of location and lifestyle; in and out of different jobs, in and out of relationships; in different cities over the years.

If there is any lingering discomfort with being 'gay', this Jungian approach has certainly offered a positive way of healing internalised homophobia.

Gay men are sometimes anti-woman, and not all drag performance is affectionate. If the relationship with the feminine in one's own psyche is embittered, it *can* be healed. Similarly, if you have been taught that you are not a 'real man', that too is being healed, surprisingly, in affirmative ways. Gay or straight; male or female ... This binary modelling is simply no longer adequate. If I may borrow John McClure's words, an emerging post-secular vision carries a sense of the world as an 'inexorable excess of being over structures of interpretation and identity' [McClure. 7].

My journey this far has been moving me from woundedness through healing. The intense period in the setting of the celibate, obedient ashram helped to shift my centre, to locate a timeless source of inspiration and strength; in a sense, allowing my anxious little self to connect with an underlying reality far deeper than my personal, angst-riddled life. From dis-location, I am re-locating a source of inspiration, one that I almost lost when my parents burned the yellow dress, forty-plus years ago. I am finding the intersection of the finite with infinite, quite close to home; within my very breath. And, even among all the daily *doing*, I have been able to put down a deep tap-root into being.

I remember that the Tokyo brothers' ashram where I stayed was in Kichijoji, an urban sub-centre known as a vibrant locus for youth culture – less for fashion, like the Shibuya and Harajuku districts – than for the music scene. The sisters' house was behind the station, overlooking the park at Inokashira-koen, where folk gather every Spring for the traditional viewing of the cherry trees' blossoming.

The brothers' house, away on the other side of the railway station, boasted a small but precious square of garden that had been wrested back from the urban overcrowding. In a windstorm, a small tree in the yard had been uprooted and it was an easy read as a metaphor for the necessity of putting down deep roots. If water is too plentiful in an area with a lot of rain, it seems that the tree's roots would never have to sink deep to find the aquifer, so when tested by a buffeting wind, thus easily succumb.

I drew out the parallel in *satsang* and then I went on to test the theory in practice. Living the ashram lifestyle had enabled me to re-join the matrix of original being, put my roots down deep into the timeless, no less; and my allotted service role helped me focus myself deeply into that process.

That was a perfect situation on many levels, and yet I still, eventually, jumped overboard! I have had to test the inner growth in understanding against 'real-world' conditions.

Civic unrest

In March 1991 a local TV news program runs video of what appears to be an assault by police officers on a black motorist. It is amateur home video, taken at night, and the first few seconds are out of focus but what soon becomes clear is that a group of police officers are hitting a man repeatedly with batons. What can he have done to deserve such a beating?

The offender is on the ground and although he is moving around, he seems submissive long before the blows cease to rain down on him. The vision is gruesome but strangely gripping – it looks like something you'd see in a corrupt, third-world dictatorship, not the land of the brave and the home of the free; and too far by far from the noble ideals of my maternal grandparents from Ohio.

A viewer by the name of George Holliday has supplied the amateur video, which is soon being played and replayed on all major media outlets nationwide. When he heard noises in the street in front of his apartment, Mr Holliday picked up his camcorder and started taping the violent beating through his window, as it unfolded in front of him. The police officers were from Foothill Police Division out in the San Fernando Valley and it seems that more than a dozen of them surrounded the offender.

Worse, the man on the ground was black and the police officers seemed for the most part to be white. After a pursuit on the Foothill Freeway during which the driver resisted being pulled over, allegedly, he was finally stopped. By the time he got out of the car there were several patrol units in attendance.

Three of the police are hitting him with batons or kicking him, while the others appear to be standing around and watching.

The LAPD is not used to having its activities caught on tape. In a reversal of conventional roles it seems that in this case the bad guys – the 'perpetrators' – might just be the police. As the vision is played over and over again on television, the public becomes convinced that the officers involved should be brought up on charges. By the time they are brought to trial, a year later, the result seems to be a foregone conclusion.

It comes as a shock then, as the verdicts are read on April 29th, 1992, that just one of the officers is found guilty of excessive force; the others are cleared of all charges. But how can that be? We have all seen the video.

As a case attracting national attention, the verdicts are broadcast live-to-air on all the major news outlets.

At the Parker Center – police headquarters, downtown LA – a small crowd becomes unruly and begin to express their anger and frustration by attacking cars at random and destroying a kind of sentry box at a security gate. This police headquarters is named after a former commander whose oppressive containment practices led directly to the explosive riots in the historic Watts district in August 1965, so there's been a history of trying to keep black folks locked down in defined areas heavily patrolled by police.

Word spreads quickly throughout the city, and rioting starts to break out here and there. For the first hour or so, citizens and authorities are unsure how bad the situation could get. Television stations break into afternoon programming, initially to take live feed of the verdict and, as the situation worsens, stay on air, casting aside their scheduled programming. Right across town people are locked on to their TV screens, anxiously trying to size up the situation.

Small fires break out amid the chaos: a liquor store here, a camera store there. With no time to get a *post hoc* grip on events, the news anchors speculate live on air, throwing out anxious questions to any official they can get to face up to a camera to make sense of the raw footage they are unleashing on us all.

Before too long, it is the outrageous attack on an individual that signals the nasty nature of what is transpiring and continues to rivet us to our screens. Even white folk feel that justice has been denied. Now we're all scared. Drivers caught in their vehicles in the wrong part of town are making U-turns to try to get around the clusters of people milling around at intersections, randomly throwing rocks and bottles at the passing cars.

The police are not visible at the trouble spots, having been ordered to pull back so as not to exacerbate the fury; for they are becoming targets themselves.

So the mob is free to vent hate on motorists who happen to find themselves in the wrong place at the wrong time. At the intersection of Florence and Normandie in South Central, a white man named Reginald Denny is pulled from his truck, repeatedly kicked and bashed senseless. One of his attackers picks up a large piece of cinder-block and throws it at the inert body, smashing him in the head. After the beating, the assailant raises his hands towards the helicopter overhead and flashes a gang sign, as he dances in gruesome celebration. Someone reaches into Denny's pocket and steals his wallet.

Civil order is crumbling before our eyes.

I'm at home, off work, only a few miles away, lying flat on my back, so I was watching television when the verdicts were read out, and I watch these events in horror. Yesterday, loading something for the office into my little car, I wrecked my back – exacerbating an old injury – and am virtually paralysed. I dragged my futon onto the floor.

Within twenty-four hours the city is brought to a standstill, and the violence and mayhem continue, day and night, for a total of three days. The TV set stays on, uninterrupted. As the situation worsens and a complete breakdown of civil order seems likely, schools and businesses are closed, Mayor Tom Bradley imposes a curfew, and California Governor Pete Wilson sends in 4,000 National Guard troops to patrol the streets.

More fires break out. They are deliberately lit. In the Watts uprising in 1965, the rioters had trashed their own neighbourhood but here there seems to be a systematic plan to spread the insurrection across a much wider map. The number of fires grows to five or six, then a dozen, then two dozen or more. They are now breaking out over a wide part of the city. Carloads of arsonists leap-frog suburbs to start conflagrations in new areas. As buildings are torched, little wisps of smoke turn to grey, then black, then erupt into orange flames, billowing forth in location after location, and when flames roll through the roof of a building, the fire spreads to adjacent structures. Whole strips of mini-malls (a feature of the Los Angeles cityscape) go up in flames.

I wonder: When this all subsides, how will people go about their daily affairs?

Firemen are prevented from responding to many of these early fires because snipers are shooting at them and police soon have to escort the firefighters for protection. The sheer number of fires, over a wide area, rapidly outstrips the capacities of the number of fire-fighting units that are available. The situation spins rapidly out of control.

Through it all, the drone of choppers hovering overhead in the smoke and haze provides a constant audio and video track for the action. Some are 'official', flying as the overwhelmed representatives of civic order, but these few are far outnumbered by the media, relaying their mixed messages through the flames. Long since having lost its sense of detached observer, Television itself becomes a breathless player in the drama. Shadowy figures on the street dart in and out of a liquor store at the corner, say, taking what they want. The looting is going on right below the choppers that are almost fanning the flames. At home viewers get live updates of what is going on in their local neighbourhoods and, pretty soon, it becomes a free-for-all.

What began as an expression of outrage soon becomes an opportunity for the have-nots to gleefully get themselves some.

Pretty much disabled, for the next thirty-six hours, I participate in events at a glassy remove, channel-surfing for the ghoulish best in pictures. The usual brainless flow of homogenized sitcoms, talk shows and commercials has been abruptly replaced, as if some giant hand grabbed all the remote controls across the city and peremptorily switched to the Reality Channel. This is happening outside, not in Bosnia, and it is television that is bringing it home, just as it did before from foreign fields on video landscapes made familiar through the one homogenized global community channel. Analysis abandoned, flushed reporters transmit breathlessly from the frontlines.

My life suspended, entranced by a stream of pictures, I am caught in a strange, chaotic convergence, as the tide of violence surges north up La Brea towards my own neighbourhood.

That 7-11 and that appliance store are just two blocks from here, yet I'd be a fool to go and look, wouldn't I?

Mine is a ground floor apartment, just a few feet back from the street and the sidewalk. The next brick shown coming through the next window needs only to come crashing through that screen for reality and its image to coincide, shaking me from my torpor, smashing the screen and hitting me right between the eyes.

Along the entire length of Hollywood Boulevard peach-skinned soldiers from the National Guard huddle together on street corners, conspicuous if nervous reminders that, finally, the law has teeth.

When the dust begins to settle, I do venture out to the nearby corner of Sunset and La Brea. A washing machine stands alone in the carpark, the last artefact dragged from an electrical appliance store, abandoned high and dry when the angry tide of looters retreated, back down La Brea. Gleaming white in the daylight, its hoses hang uselessly, unconnected. Across the deserted expanse of empty paving my local 7-11 is boarded up, opaque windows allow no looking in or out. Every other store that has them has pulled their shutters down, tight-lipped against the predations of the dispossessed. (It reminds me of that time in Seoul, South Korea in 1981, when I was finding it hard to breathe in an atmosphere choking in tear gas.)

On Monday, May 4, 1995, schools and businesses reopen and life returns to some semblance of normality. Twelve thousand people have been arrested; over four thousand have been injured; more than fifty people have died; and damage to property is estimated at more than a billion dollars.

A city still in shock takes stock after the deep disaffection simmering beneath the surface of an uneasy civil order has boiled over. At its height there was a crazy edge of glee unleashed. Now there is a dawning sense that while anarchy might be fun for a while, without some kind of order, literally everything is threatened.

The city slowly comes to its senses. In Ralph's supermarket on Sunset, there's a wary sensitivity, a new awareness of each other, with a rare degree of overt respect.

Rodney King, the victim of the alleged police brutality, plaintively asks: 'Can't we all just get along?', and while his appeal touches the heart, it points up the depth of the divisions.

At better times you'd hardly notice the tensions bubbling away below the surface. Take my 'hood, for example: Hollywood. During the week, a trashy collection of souvenir shops proffering T-shirts and kitschy movie memorabilia to the tourists. Touts offer tickets to tapings of TV shows; homeless street kids (and there are plenty) frighten the tourists before the cops harry them along. Occasionally at Mann's Chinese Theatre, just down the street, stars emerge from stretch limousines for movie premieres, to swish past the fans on red carpets, or pose for photo ops when they get their star on the Hollywood Walk of Fame.

The sidewalk from La Brea through to Vine carries these plaques; entertainment history is a series of names trodden underfoot. At night, the bitumen street surface glitters under the headlights: a city councillor has decided that Hollywood needs more glitz and has sparkle mixed with the bitumen. But roadworks inevitably dig up sections for underground works, and the grand vision is compromised.

Sunday mornings, there's a street market just off the famous Boulevard, with organic food stalls. A real village community emerges from the tacky backstreets. Small enough to do in under an hour, pleasant enough to linger. A man walks by with a vivid green iguana on his shoulder. Fresh fish, fruit, bread and vegetables. Three live musicians. Here's a dollar for the tortured blind Mexican singer whose pain unfurls in his songs. I spend my last dollar for the week on a gaudy scarf from which a costume will later emerge.

Throckmartin Farms sell all kinds of onions and garlic and the display, on fresh gingham, is a work of art. Dee Dee Bayyzk, artist, and John Throckmartin, architect, have rescued scarce varieties of antique seeds and draw much of their produce from an acre of the rarest goodies under cultivation.

For fifty cents, two middle-aged clowns give face-painting fantasies to little kids. Cheap at thrice the price, they are the works of happy hearts blowing bubbles of joy across sweet young faces wearing unique masks for a day, traveling trails of enchantment floating up the street.

There are shortbreads, home-made pasta; paper plates of Southern cooking; avocados, strawberries, home-made jams; cactuses and plants and flowers in profusion, a challenge to the dessicated identity of the Southern Californian desert spring.

This is a bizarre contrast for a city in shock, taking stock after deep-rooted disaffection has boiled over into riots, and greed and looting. There was a crazy edge of glee, like an unscheduled few days off from school, but now a dawning sense that, while anarchy is fun for a while, without some kind of order, literally everything is threatened.

The city slowly comes to its senses and in the markets, there's a wary sensitivity, a new awareness of each other, unusual respect, even the beginnings of courtesy, not to stretch the point. Survivors cling to reports of community consciousness, trade stories, share wary signs of hope.

City of (lost) angels (ii)

As prevalent as guns have become here in the Wild West, it's not always firearms that settle disputes around drug deals. Exercising at least a rudimentary awareness of common-sense precautions for self-protection, I move to an apartment on the top floor.

One of the windows in my new place upstairs looks down over the intersection of Hawthorne Avenue and North Poinsettia Place. Early one evening, a brief outburst of some muffled argument, followed by a muffled crunching noise, draws my attention to that window.

A single sneaker lies abandoned in the middle of the intersection.

A neighbour and I go down to street level to get more information. Looking west up the street we notice that the side of several cars are smeared with red paint.

Only it's not paint.

A body is slumped, lifeless, two blocks further up the street. It's the body of the 'customer' who had reached into the window of a dealer's car. Whoever was 'selling' has taken the money without handing over the drugs and abruptly accelerated away. But the dude who was buying wouldn't let go of his grip, so as they accelerated up the street, they scraped his body off against those parked cars.

Hustled!

As my lifestyle has settled into something like a routine, I venture out to the bars, hoping for a date. This is not an easy option for me, as I don't like booze, and the louche camaraderie of the smoke-filled bar scene is the last milieu in which I can ever fully relax after the focused life of the ashrams. I'm even more uptight than I was when I first went out to Chez Ivy or The Purple Onion as a nerdy grad. student in Sydney, in my early 20s. At 47 years of age, in a town where appearance is everything and youth is so highly prized, I am all but invisible. Not a bad cover, as I am about to realise …

So I am surprised when in a bar named the Gold Coast, an attractive young man offers to buy me a drink, which is uncommonly sociable of him. I have read that this is a 'cruisy' bar with an unpretentious clientèle but he is, unexpectedly, the most attractive man present.

I notice he is carrying a bag. He shares his story with me. He had to drop out of college on the East Coast after a fight with his family. He has only been in southern California for a few weeks and has just been kicked out of his temporary digs. I offer to help out with a few nights' accommodation, and he comes home with me. He's in his late twenties, with well-cut brown hair, blue-grey eyes and a light olive complexion, and his name is Rivers. From New Hampshire. There's some French connection a generation or so back. He is well spoken, with good manners.

I can hardly believe my luck. And he bought *me* a drink.

Back at my apartment we have mild, 'vanilla' sex.

In my deluded delight, for the next two days I go into full-on mothering mode. I drive him back to his previous place to pick up more of his things, lend him some cash, make sure he eats well, and so on. The whole catastrophe.

When he spends the cash on crack cocaine I am shocked; I thought that crack cocaine was a ghetto drug and he seems so well presented. When he lights up a rock I try it too. As usual, the drug offers no high that I would want to exchange my meditation experience for. But I do crave his company. I try to tell him about this beautiful natural experience already inside of him.

But, as he smokes more, he is less and less interested in me.

The evidence is clear, but do I want to see it?

Only in retrospect I can ponder: Do we really see who is before us? Do we always fall for our projections? When a user type sees me hooked on my projection, he can pull back, he can relax. That's the primal dynamic: I am looking for an intimate connection. When he doesn't meet me half-way, I go further to make up the difference; with my own need filling in the blanks. What a sucker!

The next day I notice that a watch is missing. I ask him about it and we go over to a house in East Hollywood where he promises to buy back the watch with some more cash I 'lend' him. As he doesn't want to upset the dealer by introducing a new face, he tells me to wait in the car. I slide down in the car seat with the radio playing quietly while he disappears down a back street. An hour and a half later, when he hasn't returned, I get out of the car and walk around the nearby streets but there is no sign of him.

It's not the most salubrious part of Hollywood and I have no idea which of these houses huddled in the night was his intended destination. So I go home in a mood of disappointment mixed with disgust. Next morning I go to work, as usual, hoping that nothing bad has happened to him.

Two days later, he turns up back at my apartment, needing a shower. Of course, there's no watch.

Apologetic, he is the model of contrition. I feel awkward, suddenly cast as a kind of parent figure when I had expected a companion.

He seems like a kid from a good family, gone briefly off the rails and, as he pleads his case, together we imagine a different future for him. He begs for some private time (I guess he wants to smoke some crack). He takes my keys to sit in my car in the underground carpark, not realising that I am now pretty much locked in to my high security building, so I have to wait for him to return. My mood sours.

He later gives me a letter that he has written on the back of a receipt for an auto battery service he found in the glove box of my car. The writing looks immature to me, with only elementary punctuation, and each line slides off the page:

Victor, I really don't know what to say, as I do this I think back to whenever my mother and I would have disagreements and I was at fault, I could always put my true feelings on paper.

So, I have become his mother!

When we were together last night I felt something that hit me. I'm finally realizing that maybe you are what I need, what I want, when you were talking about young men having to have love and guidance from an older man I knew exactly what you were saying. I never got that from my dad. You give me confidence and make me feel good about myself. I know that this could be just what we've been looking for, for both of us. But there is a dark shadow over this whole thing, I know now I have a problem with crack.

That's promising.

I'm willing to take the proper steps to end this chaos. What I need to know is if you are willing to help me. But I'll understand if your [sic] not and you would rather just continue on without me. But I just know that this could work. We just have to want it to happen. Sometimes I don't act like it or seem as if I feel the way you do, it's just that I have a hard time expressing my feeling and emotion and I'm praparing [sic] myself for a commitment. I guess what I am saying is I'm leaving it in your hands. I want to make it work, I think we can be happy together, were just going to have to put some effort into it.

I'm charmed. I introduce him to my best friend Susan, who bristles with suspicion. She has had an affair with a young wannabe rocker, who abused weed and speed and has previously spent time as a live-in lover with a female studio executive who kept him in great style. But Susan grew up in New York, and she knows the ropes far better than I do; I don't realise how gullible I am. Her withering scorn cuts through my romantic projections, seeing past Richard's clean-cut appearance to ask: 'What is he doing with his life?'

Richard doesn't follow through on my idealistic dream plan. He effectively strings me along for two more days, with no more love-making, even of the vanilla variety, while he's waiting for a phone call from a well-to-do gentleman who has promised to take him on holiday to Cabo St. Lucas in Baja California, which doesn't seem like a very constructive option, long term, to me.

When that hoped-for call doesn't transpire, he turns his charms on me. But I'm not really interested and he goes into the bathroom, presumably to jack off alone. I am still trying to find some kind of constructive way forward for him and I offer him some work clipping technology stories from my stack of national newspapers, which I search for stories with potential for television that might transfer to the show I'm working on. No matter what the distractions of my so-called 'personal' life I must keep up my workload.

I farm out some clipping work like this to people within our own office who need to make some extra money, so I switch it his way, briefing him about the kind of stories I am looking for. It's a small task, but I figure it would be better to be spending money he has earned than to rely on hand-outs. While I'm still being paid by the Australians I have little money to share. Romance or not, I have to be practical.

As he is completely broke, he needs the money upfront, of course, so I pay him in advance.

I go off to work, leaving him alone in the apartment with a stack of papers, some scissors and some food, hoping that when I come back in the evening he will have recognized the value of earning money from his own labours.

I get back from work around 6.30 p.m. The front door is ajar, and the sliding door to the balcony is open. There is no sign of my house guest, and the pile of papers has not been touched. Perhaps he has just slipped out for a moment …

When he has not returned by midnight I meditate, lock up, and go to bed.

Next morning, suspicion kicks my brain into another gear and I get up and start checking my belongings. My favourite jacket is missing and a pair of shoes. An Australian credit card, which I have not been using in LA, has been flushed out of its hiding place and a department store card is also missing. By now it is becoming clear that he has gone.

The microwave oven is destroyed. Apparently, he heated up some leftovers in the saucepan, unaware that metal in microwaves is fatal.

In order to weave a plausible scenario I try to find some threads from among scraps of paper he has left behind. There's a phone number on one of these scraps and someone I haven't met says he saw Robert yesterday who told him that he was 'going to Hawaii'. I call the department store and report my card stolen and try to call Australia to put a stop on the missing credit card as well. It's a little difficult because Friday in LA is already Saturday down under.

I go into research mode and check hotels in Hawaii, working out that he will be registered in my name, as he will be using my card.

On Sunday, the credit card company in Sydney calls me at home to tell me that someone using the card in Honolulu has been detained at the airport. They had put an immediate stop on payments and when he came down to the lobby of his very expensive hotel in Waikiki, the desk clerk declined the card and withheld it. He jumped into a taxi with his girlfriend (yes, a girlfriend!) and sped out to the airport, where he was arrested by the police. The very day I thought he was becoming an honest worker, doing some clipping work for me, he went on a spending spree at Bullocks, charging more than $1100 worth of goods, including luggage. He bought two *first class* air tickets to Hawaii and when he got there, he bought an expensive Movado watch in a gift store.

By the time I ring them on Monday the police in Honolulu have released him for 'lack of evidence'. He is passing himself off as me, with no I.D. other than a credit card and a business card in my name that he also filched. I find out from them that he has a warrant out for his arrest in his home state for passing a forged cheque, but the Honolulu police advise that they don't extradite to the East Coast. The local police in Hollywood are less than interested, with a rather witless junior officer citing 'double jeopardy' and saying that as Robert has been in my home with my permission, I should just let it go.

It has been an expensive lesson in various ways, even though the credit companies don't hold me responsible for most of it.

I feel foolish. The intimacy promised in his charming note has not materialised.

Why do I get the sense that I've been doing *all* the work in this *faux* relationship? I haven't yet understood that a hustler mentality quickly recognises how to play this fool.

At my age, I really shouldn't be so naïve.

But I miss the irony altogether. It strikes me, only much later, that in all my detective efforts trying to track down his whereabouts – ringing hotels asking if someone with my name is staying there – that I have been, virtually, *looking for myself*. The only ID he has is a credit card and an out-of-date business card, *in my name*.

A few months later, a couple of friends I know from my television days in Melbourne come through town and crash on the floor (and sofa) of my apartment. As we catch up with each other's news, of course I tell them about my misadventure with the handsome hustler. At the end of their visit, they take me out to a restaurant up on Sunset Strip where we share a bottle of wine to go with the California cuisine as we enjoy the passing parade from our table out on the sidewalk.

As we get up to go, I happen to look inside the main part of the restaurant. I have been sitting with my back to a curved section, all glass, which gives a fishbowl view of the interior. There, sitting at a table for two, complete with bottle of wine and an ice bucket is a young suit – probably a middle level executive in the music recording, or television, or film industry – and his dinner companion, I see, is none other than Robert Rivers.

They have been there for the entire duration of our meal and Robert has obviously caught sight of me already. His face is flushed, he is drinking heavily and talking too much. His date can't figure out why his behaviour is so flustered. I see all this in an instant.

I mention to my friends that the guy who ripped me off several months earlier is inside the restaurant.

'What are you going to do?' they chorus.

We pause and look through the main window. His discomfort is so acute that it's all I can do not to double up with laughter. I need do no more to spoil his fun – my presence alone has been enough to unsettle him and ruin his evening. Perhaps he has been imagining that I would storm in there to confront him; denounce him to his dinner date as a hustler (and a jailbird). But my amusement is more than adequate compensation in the *schadenfreude* department.

'What do you expect me to do?' I explain to my friends, as I lead the way back to the car. 'He was my teacher!'

Postcards from the edge

It's not all work, work, work. I get invited to an afternoon party out in Topanga Canyon, where I meet up with Ellie Bambridge, an old premie friend from Melbourne, who is visiting LA with her intriguing partner Timothy Wyllie. Timothy is a Scottish architect who is building a sustainable house out in the desert country of New Mexico and Ellie has been helping him. I had a brief holiday with them in New Mexico, between jobs last year, where certain strange occurrences disturbed my sense of everyday reality.

Somewhere along the line, Timothy took a left turn and never returned to the life of social convention. Tall, with long grey-white hair, to me he looks like the wizard Gandalf from Tolkien's *Lord of the Rings*. He is a highly intelligent and independent thinker who has written books about telepathy with dolphins, as well as water birthing, and angels. He likes to dress sometimes as 'Georgia', a kind of female alter ego. He is quite serious about communicating with extraterrestrials and fond of navigating parallel universes with the help of various chemicals.

It's a fine day in the Canyon and we're out in the garden, standing by a pond, observing the movement of some fat orange-white *koi*. Suddenly, the fish notice our attention and they flick away, partly concealing themselves under some water plants.

I wonder what it would be like to suddenly become aware of the presence of a 'higher' life form, from another dimension, paying attention to me.

I've been talking with Timothy and Ellie about their work, running workshops based on a book he has co-written about 'contacting your angels'. This is a matter of fact for them, and I feel a twinge of envy. Yes, envy! I am something of a clodhopper is such contexts.

Next morning, I go into work and, while sitting at my desk, I am brushed on the shoulder by a postcard that flutters down from the pin-board above my chair. That's odd. Of all the things attached to the board, why has this one brushed me this morning?

It's a photo of a painting I admired on a visit to Italy. In Firenze I had broken off from my travelling party to spend a few hours in the Uffizi gallery. We had been in Rome for an event with my Teacher and travelled north. In Siena, we had arrived almost by accident during the enchanting street festival in December celebrating the shortest day of the year; the festival of Santa Lucia.

While I'm not particularly enamoured with religious iconography, this painting was the one souvenir I had bought on leaving the Uffizi, just to remind me of the brilliant collections housed there. For example, I was stunned by the sheer size of the 15th Century Botticelli *Birth of Venus*, more than any of the various Madonnas with child. This postcard featured another work by an obscure artist, that focuses on 'the annunciation'.

It isn't the one ascribed to Leonardo da Vinci and his painting master Andrea del Verrocchio, nor the Fra Angelico, but a more formal work, with arches, and the side-on, almost frieze-like posing of the figures, suggesting an earlier period. By Duccio di Buoninsegna perhaps? I don't think so; and it's not the Domenico Veneziano; certainly not the Strozzi, nor the Neri di Bicci, which is in another Gallery.

I pause to pin it back up on the board and get back to work. Maybe a cleaner has taken it down to admire it and not pinned it up properly?

Some weeks later, this time by phone, I notice that I'm feeling sorry for myself, as if I'm lacking the sensitivity to feel the presence of such supernatural beings, with whom Timothy and Ellie seem to be intimately acquainted. But when I come into work again next morning, there it is again, sitting in my chair!

Now I'm not one to reach out for extra-human aid; my Teacher has worked to help me find a pragmatic connection from within. And that's why I try to centre myself inside in a formal meditation practice, every day. At the very least, beginning at the beginning helps me keep my balance. I know that my breath is a gift, the one source that enables me to be, here, at this time, in fact. But, resting in that point of balance, these hints abound that the Universe in which I live is fascinating and more complex than my prosaic understanding would normally allow. 'Reality' doesn't stop at the border of my brain, or my skull, or my conceptual framework, just because I'm not paying attention. And, while I have an ingrained resistance to Christian iconography, the birth of the Christ child is a potent symbol; coming at me as a 'postcard from the edge' to hint to me of parallel experiences of re-birth that I am going through, so often spontaneously and marked as synchronously as these postcards would seem to indicate.

Paramount Studios, Melrose Ave, Hollywood

I'm toiling in television production, an anonymous cog in the wheels of an industry that churns out dreams for international mass consumption. Hollywood, the Maya factory. They play re-runs of *I Love Lucy* in Bali! The production office is on the Paramount lot on Melrose Avenue. When I line up for food at the commissary I am joined by actors from *Star Trek: The Next Generation*, in full make-up and costume, with those oddly constructed foreheads, ears and noses.

I have moved beyond *Beyond 2000* to work the medical desk on a tabloid news magazine show, pumping out stories on the latest diets, diseases, and drugs (mostly of the pharmaceutical variety, but I must be alert for stories about the latest party drugs too). I pitch stories to the producers and follow up on the ones that fit their sometime enigmatic requirements. 'Following up' means trying to gather enough background for a research file on the story, line up people to interview and pass them on to a production manager to arrange crews to shoot elements of the story and the essential interviews. I try to direct these shoots from my desk, in the newsroom. With all the elements in place, the stories are usually moved along to specialist writer types to work up for broadcast and then on to one of the on-camera personalities (who may have had little to do with the story) to present on camera.

I'm juggling up to a dozen stories on the go.

In the mornings I float through the security gates in a walking meditation, trying to maintain a state of equilibrium from my early meditation practice at home. I need to feel the independence of that innate bliss nature carrying me, for during a day of urgent deadlines and the anxious search for stories that no-one else will find, I know I will lose touch with the bliss! No matter how calm I feel at the beginning I will surely be wrung out by the end of the day. The obsessive focus on things that don't ultimately matter is a grinding reality and, as much as I can, I try to hold all that at bay. It's as if I'm here, but not really here; and sometimes the attempt at maintaining detachment isn't working.

I park my car in the assigned lot and I cross the road to enter through the security check on Gower, at the western edge of the Paramount lot. I'm heading in to work on Sound Stage 26, feeling the peace breathing from the deep embrace of this morning's practice still holding me. But no matter how much I will try to stay connected with this peace, after ten hours on the job I will be run ragged, and my careful equanimity will be sorely tested. Stress is no substitute for the calm benefits of inner peace, even if the money is good.

At the end of the day (or after midnight; whenever I make my escape) I will drive slowly back to my new apartment in West Hollywood and, before I even think about preparing food, I simply sit, letting the tensions of the day fall away so I can recover the peaceful core of being that I left behind someplace, during the maddening day.

Stage 26 has been adapted into a newsroom with a small, attached studio where they record the hostings of the show. Beside us on Stage 26 is the large studio for the *Leeza* show audiences. Across the road lies our research department and a workroom that hums all day and night as field tapes are logged for transcripts; (some of the most interesting people moonlight here). Upstairs are the offices for *Entertainment Tonight*. To the other side, across a laneway, is the studio where *Frasier* is recorded. Kelsey Grammer's Bentley has an exclusive parking space alongside. Sometimes you'll meet the dog, and one or another of the actors.

The newsroom is a busy environment, intensely focused, driven and noisy. Twenty-five or more people working in a mostly open plan situation, with multiple phones ringing, questions shouted and answered across the space. The nerve centre of the newsroom is the assignment desk, where small teams on 24-hour rotation monitor various newsfeeds, news wires and so on; doling out stories, assigning reporters and crews.

I'm one of the types hired to chase up my own leads and pitch ideas to a number of senior producers. If I don't have enough balls in the air at any one time, I might get thrown a lead from the assignment desk, often involving some bogus celebrity, those types whom they take way too seriously, in my book, but this is Hollywood. So I try to come up with original stories that are of interest to me at least, in order to sidestep the garbage.

They're also keeping their eyes on multiple TV monitors to catch the news feeds from the East Coast as well as stations right across LA County. This bank of monitors may randomly get turned up loud when everyone's favourite news event, apparently – namely, high-speed car chases involving police pursuits – is being monitored, LIVE! by more and more stations as the word gets out. If there's one police chopper on the job, you can bet there will be another four or five hovering noisily overhead to capture shots for news coverage. Stations break into regular programming to be first on air with the latest outrage.

Most newsworthy events leave me cold – I have my own stories to set up and follow through, dammit! – until one day the humdrum of everyday crises is interrupted by the mother of all car chases. And this one will not be ignored. I'm working in a newsroom so it will be pushed right into my workspace.

A famous former college footballer, one Orenthal J. Simpson, is heading south on the 405 freeway, attempting to escape police who are investigating him on suspicion for the murder of his former wife (a blonde beauty named Nicole, a trophy wife for an African American success story) and a male friend of hers, in the entrance way to her apartment in Brentwood, an upscale part of town between Hollywood and the ocean. 'OJ' is a folk hero, and his long-drawn-out arrest as a suspect in relation to the murders instantly achieves wide national coverage. Our news program will cover the investigation, as well as the subsequent trial through all its dramatic stages.

As the live coverage via helicopter tracks the progress of a white SUV south, via both news and police choppers, people gather on freeway overpasses to cheer their sporting legend on, as if he were heading for another touchdown. Speculation has it that the drive south is no innocent outing but a frantic attempt to cross the Mexican border down near San Diego. Adding to the drama, it is reported that OJ is holding a gun to his head. With a number of police vehicles and choppers patiently tracking his progress, OJ and his driver are eventually forced to give up the attempt as futile, and they circle back towards his home in Brentwood, where he is finally arrested.

Quickly the newsroom is flooded with extra staff, covering every angle of the story, and it continues for months, right through and beyond his trial, his acquittal, and a subsequent civil case brought by Nicole's outraged family. Feelings among the black community are still simmering after the outrage of the acquittal of police officers beating Rodney King, and the poor behaviour of white investigators in the hunt for evidence against Simpson further alienates that community.

Rather than being tried on the west side of town where the murders occurred, empanelling a jury downtown results in a preponderance of black jurors, many of whom are women. It doesn't take much to turn them against the prosecutors' case, even as women, because here is a black brother, and a hero at that, being 'framed' by white investigators. Race trumps murder in the justice stakes. He is famous, and he is successful; apparently a role model for upwardly mobile African Americans seething with deep-seated anger from centuries of oppression.

Eventually, when the verdict of not guilty is read out in court, on live TV, the assembled throng in our newsroom are stunned into silence. Only two of us – the black female reporter and I – are not surprised. The rest of the (white) women working the show are stunned. As women, their sense of security against potential attack from aggressive men is left badly shaken. They have worked the story obsessively for months and followed every twist and turn in the evidence. Details of the testimony have been discussed all over the city. OJ's team have run rings around the prosecution.

But even when Nicole's parents sue him in a civil case, and win, it remains doubtful that the damages awarded will ever be collected.

Such are the tremors that rumble through the newsroom, holding everyone in their thrall … at least until the next outrage must be covered.

Compared to the deep peace of meditation, I sometimes feel like I am working in hell. Long black drapes hang down from the high ceiling of the sound stage cum newsroom; and the raggedy grey carpet is in poor condition, with rumours of rodents drawn to the 'craft services' food table where people graze all day and into the night, during different shifts. Phones ring loudly at unattended desks. Trying to do a pre-interview with a story contact in the middle of the din can be very difficult, especially when I am trying to ascertain the emotional impact on the lives of people in a story.

Often, after starting at 8 am, I will be thrown someone else's story to edit and at 4pm must begin another shift in an edit suite, working with an editor to compile a story with footage that I have had little time to preview. This means more money for me, as this kind of work must be paid at union rates (through the Directors' Guild), and I am in my usual state of impoverishment, especially after buying into the condo market myself and paying the hefty fees to join the Guild.

People working around me are often in a state of emotional drama, even some of the highly paid on-camera reporters in the middle of a meltdown as their deadlines loom. I long for peace and quiet. But in that setting, I can't just stand back and act as though it all has nothing to do with me; I am engaged within the maelstrom, like it or not, or my stories will fall in a heap (so my meditation practice is always highly motivated). I hope that some carry-over from the deep centering practices will keep me upright in the storm. Sometimes I'm in the shrouded newsroom before the sun rises and when I leave it's already after dark. If I allow myself to feel miserable, I could easily get depressed. Already juggling my own stories, pressures of a new story push everything onto a back burner, even those almost ready to go, while I scramble to get something else on air. My ability to be flexible is sorely tested.

But it's here, in the middle of this virtual hell that I come to realise something that will stand me in the best possible stead, now and in years to come.

The image comes to mind of a well, sitting on the outskirts of a village, fed by an underground spring. Originally the well is an important centre of village life, its waters essential for daily necessities. But, as times change, and technology produces different ways of living as a more and a more sophisticated metropolis grows up, the well is de-centred, to be gradually forgotten in favour of dazzling new substitutes – Coca Cola, 7-Up, whiskey sodas, martinis, cosmopolitan cocktails and sugary health drinks ...

Over time, the well is gradually neglected and left to collapse in on itself.

Clearing out the rubble, on the other hand, and repairing the broken-down walls reveals that, despite the neglect, the spring that originally fed the well has not disappeared. It bubbles away underground. Its waters still have the original nature, to potentially slake the thirst.

This image is relevant to my situation. Paradoxically, the stronger the delusional concerns of the frantic newsroom, the more deeply I must connect with the core experience I have spent decades uncovering within, and it is in this desperate environment that I am surprised to find myself experiencing a kind of resilience, even a state of muted joy. For when all the virtual substitutes are revealed to be illusory, the natural quality of life itself, which has always been present in the background, is recovered ... as joy. Come deeper, it insists, remember your natural self.

If I'm not always with it, it is always still there.

No matter how powerful are the stories that drive this mania, the original qualities of the source self are a sustaining peace and quiet, an irrepressible joy that nourishes my deepest core self. And it has not been by maintaining a condescending distance, nor by refusing to enter into the fray, that I can recover this source. Paradoxically it's only under this kind of intense pressure that I learn to see through the Maya and recall the value of this inner awareness as a core experience!

And that well of peace exists in every heart.

If I am not rooted in that centre, the dramas of daily living and working rob me of everything. Even if it's after hours I know the real possibility of a deep centre of abiding calm as the core of being. Perhaps it's something of that that I bring to the work, even when I'm starting to feel frazzled.

I book-end my day with the meditation practices and, for some reason, in spite of my practice of detachment, the bosses keep me on the show.

Meetings with remarkable women (cont.)

Cathay Circle, Los Angeles, circa 1995

'No, that's not the real title is it?'

I am standing in the doorway of a house in Cathay Circle. The place is owned by an older Jewish lady, Henrietta Bernstein, who has hosted a series of lectures being delivered by an intense psychic woman named Cheri, and the series, lasting over several weeks, has now come to an end.

Most of the other attendees have left but, on my way out, Henrietta stops me to ask what I 'do'. I tell her that I work on a TV program ... She interrupts me:

'Yes, but that's not all, is it?'

So I mention that in my own time I've been slowly working up a sort of memoir, a loosely-assembled story of the key incidents – including the highs and the lows – that I have experienced in my life. One of the benefits of going to classes at IGLE has been to start work on an early version of this account and this part-time project is benefiting from being taken more or less seriously in a supportive environment. One workshop is run by Elizabeth Vargas, who has been published by Virago Press; another by the award-winning Bernard Cooper, on the art of the personal essay. Both are very useful because we all have to come up with something to share for each session, and I'm still trying to sort out how to turn these incidents into some sort of shape that might be of interest to a reader.

Finding out who we are has been described as the existential research program that we're all concerned with and, as our sense of identity is informed by memory, this emerging urge to write about it in the genre of memoir will become strikingly appropriate for me.

'And what's that called?' Henrietta asks.

I tell her it's called *Child's Play*. That's what I've used as my working title, and it refers to the second scene where, as a young boy, I used to play alone, dressed in my mother's yellow dress, in the quiet room of the house.

Henrietta suggests that isn't the real name at all and asks what the title should really be.

'Um ... It's called *The Boy in the Yellow Dress*,' I say, for the first time owning what it's about, even to myself. (Maybe she'll think I'm a transvestite!) Henrietta doesn't know me but she has adroitly flushed me out of my customary hiding place. As a queer boy I learned to survive and it didn't do to assert my point of view against the run-of-the-mill consensus reality.

'Yes, that's the real title, isn't it?' she affirms with calm authority. And she explains: 'Not just about the dress.'

She hasn't finished, and I'm paying full attention now.

'Between lives, your service was to aid children in making their transitions who had died prematurely. As you approached them, they saw you in your body of light as a golden dress ...'

I am struck virtually dumb. How is it that the nudge towards growth can come from such unexpected sources?

Tracking down that damned elusive boson

April 2000, closing in on my 55th birthday. I'm between jobs and wondering what the hell I might be doing next. I go to see a film that is set in Tibet, with a Buddhist monk as a central character. He must help his village get its only tradeable commodity to market, for the benefit of all the community; but that requires carrying it across the mountains in the snow, fording icy rivers, avoiding tricky ice on the mountain trails. It's the worst possible season to be making this journey, but he has no choice.'

All in all, it is quite a spartan viewing experience.

The central lesson expressed by the monk is that when you have come to the point of making a choice between one path or another, it is important that you always choose the most challenging option. Frankly, at this point in my life I am heartily sick and tired of challenges. The very word itself brings on the shudders in my reluctant mind/body/spirit. But see what happens …

I'm using this break to get into a cleansing fast, which I've been practising under the guidance of an experienced naturopathic doctor, Timothy Brantley, a close acquaintance of my old friend, Susan Peters. I could never have taken this on except with his guidance (and her encouragement). I hear that Dr. Timothy and his colema boards are in great favour among self-styled 'supermodels', getting in shape for their next shoots. I'm no model, but I've done a couple of these fasts before and I could certainly provide a testimonial about their deep cleansing benefits.

It's not a dry fast. There are twice-daily freshly squeezed vegetable juices, lots of purified water and Timothy's own brand of digestive enzymes and cleansing herbs. You lead into the regime for at least a couple of weeks, with raw foods, and taper off the same way. I learn how to do daily colonic irrigations at home (hence the colema board), and on about the fourth of say six or seven days, an overnight 'liver and gall bladder flush'. I won't bore you with the details, but after the stunning results first time around, I look forward to this! I've truly become a Southern Californian.

One day, standing in line to collect my fresh vege juice at Erewhon whole foods market on Beverly Boulevard, I get into a discussion with a suave, handsome man, also waiting for his juice. We compare notes about whether or not to include some raw garlic in the mix. Only later do I realise that I have just had the classic Hollywood experience – a 'celebrity sighting' – but I didn't recognise who it was; he was too short. And by not gushing, I have behaved impeccably. It would have been totally uncool to act unseemly.

During my refreshing break, my dear friend Greg Vogel contacts me, asking if I could come in for a meeting with some guys he works with who have started a TV production company. Greg has been researching potential stories for a series they want to make. He asks me to share what I know about making a show full of science stories, from my time working at *Beyond 2000* and *Beyond Tomorrow*. I am in the midst of one of those juice fasts. Without going into the details, at the end of this time, I feel as high as could be, and my face and skin tend to look – how shall I say it – radiant. I am overflowing with energy and enjoy chatting with these guys.

A couple of days later, Greg calls to tell me: 'You're hired!'

'Hired? What do you mean? That was a job interview?' Crikey.

Well, I am in dire need of some income, and so I agree to check it out. The show is to be called *Science at the Edge*. Scientific research at the extremes. Fascinating material.

The principals of Greg's company are impressed by the record of that show I worked on for several years and while I am aware that I was just a small cog in that operation, these guys have assumed that I know the whole gestalt.

I know little of how this new company operates and I am not clear about their expectations. But I guess I'll find out. This seems to be one of those choices the Buddhist monk recommends. Take the hard option? I'll start at the beginning and take it one day at a time.

Besides, it's not the first time I've learned a job by doing it.

I feel stretched from day one. I'm to take a crew on the road in Europe.

While the stories certainly fit the brief: big in concept, they are not necessarily big on compelling imagery. At *Beyond*, when we would do stories with large operations like NASA, they would provide great footage, free of charge, and graphic animations to help 'tell' the story in pictures. What do you do when the story is highly theoretical? You talk to experts who explain the research. But you can't just make a story out of talking heads, and if they have dull personalities and can only talk in dense technical jargon, you always rely on your reporter to summarise, pithily, what it's all about and use fragments as quotes to string the reporter's re-telling along. But we won't be using a reporter, apparently; and I'll be the one doing the faceless interviews … In two languages!

Yes, as we're planning to sell the show in different markets, wherever possible we will provide at least some of the content in languages suiting a multicultural viewership. So, when I do an interview, at first in English, I have to get the subject to repeat the responses to my questions, all over again in their own lingo. I've prepared questions to draw out the key facts in the research.

Even in my naïveté it should have been obvious to me that this small company is heavy at the top and thin at the bottom, where I operate. And when we hit the road, I will be juggling several tasks. Including *carnets*, for Customs. Every time we cross a border we have to provide a detailed list of every single item of equipment – which is quite lengthy – coming in to, and leaving, each country.

Just as we're getting ready to fly to Paris, one of the bosses slices a day off the schedule. This means that what we have to cover in our first stop must be compressed. We're doing three stories in Paris. Then the stringer who meets us has not ordered the vehicle we requested. He's a one-man band, used to traveling with a small camera, flying in to do news reports with no crew. The message has not got through to him that we are carrying a lot of gear.

I have to deal with the *carnets*. I can get by with my literary French and, behind the jaded attitude, the Customs official is mildly amused, and proceeds to stamp the required documentation without even a perfunctory attempt to check off each item against the list. Instead of being impressed, not only by my wrangling the equipment through Customs and back to the vehicle, the cameraman is pissed off with me

... I won't go on but you'll guess that I am soon getting into quicksand and will be struggling from day to day, hour by hour, to cope with the daily demands.

I'm dizzy with those demands. And I am getting very little sleep. In addition to checking travel arrangements, keeping in mind some of the crew members' specific seating requests, making sure that there is food and water at appropriate times, changing currency, running a petty cash budget, calling ahead to confirm upcoming stories, all on top of wrangling the sometimes abstruse interviews.

In some places, where I would rely on the local 'fixer' to do the driving, I am required to be the driver, too. And every time we cross a border I have to go through the rigmarole with Customs officials and the *carnets* ... the list goes on.

A certain amount of stress can spur me to rise to the occasion but there's a point beyond which I am barely coping. Let's just say that the situation does not improve. And a key member of the crew sits back, coolly critical, offering little creative input. Each night he reports back to home base in Los Angeles (and I will get blamed about the costs of the rented phone calls). Following the three stories in different locations in Paris, the main story in Switzerland will be the worst.

We fly in to Zurich and first shoot a story on an artificial blood substitute at a blood bank in a major hospital. Tomorrow, we will drive on to Geneva to shoot requirements for a story on the 'Higgs boson', at the huge international research facility, CERN – the *Conseil Européen pour la Récherche Nucléaire*. Again, the local fixer has ignored our request to book a suitably sized van, and the crew of course blames me.

In Geneva, for the first part of the Higgs boson story I interview a scientist – a brilliant Viennese woman who had chosen to work as an astrophysicist rather than pursuing a promising career as a concert pianist – and I do my best to work through an interview in English, then repeat the questions, watching out for the key points during her responses in German, to interpose the next, and so on. Simple, right?

We'll travel back across the border by car into France this afternoon to pick up shots for the rest of the story at the main facility of CERN where the Large Hadron Collider is located and then return to Geneva tonight. This will require checking *carnets* at the customs office as we leave Switzerland and cross the road to the French customs office for checking the *carnets*, then continue the drive out to the location, now in French territory (and go through the whole rigmarole in reverse when we come back at night).

The Large Hadron Collider, the largest particle accelerator ever built, is a 9 km drive from Geneva, and located under the countryside between France and Switzerland. It's a major tool for research into particle physics. As an accelerator, it sends sub-atomic particles at high speeds around its underground tunnel to crash into each other to see if even smaller particles are formed that can be detected; basically, they're trying to re-create the conditions of the Big Bang at the earliest stage after it occurred. I'm not surprised to learn that India, as one of the countries involved as part of this huge international research consortium have provided a statue of Hindu Lord Siva, creator and destroyer of the Universe.

A little bit of theory will be required here, cadged from various research articles on particle physics that I have been reading and trying to grasp. Anything I don't understand I will try to have the scientist explain for me and for our viewers in turn, if the story ever makes it to air. If I understand it correctly, they are trying to provide a complete description of the natural world down to scales on the order of one-thousandth the size of the nucleus of an atom.

The model they are working from is a hypothetical quantum field that is ubiquitous throughout the universe, a field that is supposed to be responsible for giving particles their mass; this one is called the 'Higgs' field. All quantum fields are said to have a fundamental particle associated with them and this one is the boson, hence, the 'Higgs boson'.

Obviously, it's hard to observe these sub-atomic particles with the naked eye, hence the construction and use of this massive particle accelerator that we are visiting today. Trying to confirm the theoretical edifice of particle physics involves some rather large hardware, which will at least give us something large enough to shoot with our camera. The major shortfall is that we don't have a reporter who appears on camera and explains the story. The people back at home base have decided to do without one. The main thing to avoid is lots of talking heads where the 'talent', or the expert, is on screen explaining everything.

I assume that we will make great use of additional footage provided by the people whose project we are working on, which would be edited into the story. Normally, I assume we will be able to rely on simple graphics, too, to illustrate something we can't shoot. Otherwise, how to turn these various areas of scientific research *at the edge* into stories we can tell on television? These issues leave a growing list to be followed up in post-production, a department that will have to be developed back in LA when and if we finally return with plenty of footage of interviews, at least.

Obviously, I'm out of my depth here (not only in scientific terms but also in the direction of each day's shoot) but when has that ever stopped me? However, this is more than, say, being thrown in the deep end of the pool and struggling to float, or dogpaddle, to the edge. Surrounded by a cynical crew and sceptical management back in LA, my best efforts are little better than dogpaddle.

Why do I get the feeling that I have been set up to fail?

We travel on and cover two more stories in England, but the sinking feeling deepens apace. I realise that there is a lot more to go to make these stories work and I have failed miserably to compensate, on the run. Sincerity is not enough when a certain level of competence is *de rigueur*, from my side, and a sophisticated production apparatus adequate to the vision of the company's bosses, on their side.

You've guessed it. When I drag myself back to home base in LA they leave it up to my friend Greg to tell me my time is up. While I feel that I've failed to meet the expectations of his colleagues, more than that, I've let Greg down. It's a similar experience to the time when John Young let me go from *Young Talent Time*. I see the lips moving and, even while I know I should be feeling one way, on the inside I am relieved … to leave!

Outright failure is still an awful feeling to juggle in my state of psychological turmoil.

It seems that naïveté is not an adequate excuse; but what was this all about? In Paris, we have covered the story of an atomic clock getting the measurement of a second down to the finest degree; a space-based platform for a telescope system that will enable scientists to look further into space (and back in time); and peered deeper into sub-atomic events at CERN; a blood substitute technology in Zurich; an analysis of core samples from deep ice in Antarctica (in Cambridge). From deep space to subatomic particles; from the length of a second, to that moment just after the 'Big Bang' …

I have developed a great respect for scientists and the extraordinary range of scientific inquiry, but in an unguarded moment, in a lull in the interview with the dazzling scientist at CERN, I remember asking her: 'But what was there, *before* the 'Big Bang'?'

I recall my Teacher's reminder that when we are looking for signs of life 'out there', are we missing the obvious life we are living here, and what it is that makes this all possible, the sine qua non for our own existence? If science can penetrate the mystery of being and consciousness here, now, let me shoot the story of *that* inquiry.

I will ponder this entire experience for several decades, probing and poking at it, like a torturous Zen *mondo*. As I revisit the memory I have to look beyond my disappointment and the sense of personal failure to recognise something here pointing to a meaning that eludes me … Something about developing the intense inquiry into the inner life – consciousness itself – with a level of passion and finesse matching the ambition and dedication of these scientists' worthy pursuits.

Shingles (or, crocodile skin?)

Often my body lets me down. Sometimes, on the treadmill of churning out stories I only half believe in, I literally, 'get the shits'. But I am not sufficiently attentive to get 'the message' from down under. With the prolonged pressure of newsroom deadlines it's easy to ignore and override the signals my body is sending out. Will my body become an increasingly uncomfortable residence; unreliable when I need it to just persevere? Yet ... all the while I am with it, it remains my vehicle, perhaps even my laboratory?

When the newsroom closes down, I feel forced to seek more work.

Then Susan offers me work on a new show, called *House Calls*, which follows home visits by a Canadian psychiatrist to families in crisis. The pay is good, and I'm offered work through to Christmas. It doesn't take me long to size up how to edit up the little packages required, but the pressure to do more and more grows to the point where I'm expected to work for six or even more days a week ...

After Thanksgiving, November 2000

Lying around my apartment, shirtless. No, I won't say 'laying'; I'm not a bird depositing eggs. But, even writing 'lying', I'm virtually 'lying', in another sense, for I'm in such discomfort that I have to invent new angles of repose, semi-upright, to get any so-called 'rest'.

This spartan regime has been imposed by an intense bout of shingles. And it's been going on *for weeks*!

Shingles. It sounds like roof-tiling. Sections of my skin are coarse enough, but I'd have to look up an etymological dictionary to see if there's a link in language. Long periods of wakefulness might allow such trivial pursuits, and the pain is so relentless I need the distraction, but I am without energy and word games are wearisome. Spent. If I manage to do the washing I lack the energy to make the bed.

It's January, and the Los Angeles winter is mild, so I don't have to deal with clothing. Overnight a light cotton sarong, loosely draped, is all I need. It's actually really difficult to lie down. Areas affected include the right side of my face, right up into the hairline, down my throat and neck, across the top of my back to the right shoulder, down my arm and spreading across the right side of my chest. I prop myself precariously on part of my left side, but the upper quadrant is a no-go zone. I spend hours in a state of light meditation (and an equal time sitting playing computer games). Where should I park my attention, otherwise, when I can't find the off-switch for pain ... To all physical sensation?

My body has betrayed me.

It feels like the nerve endings under my skin have been fried. And there's no relief, day or night. Maybe burn victims feel like this. It is a bad case.

It's not supposed to last this long. I know, because when I finally got to see a skin specialist the week after Thanksgiving, and he eventually gave up trying to treat me, I knew I was in for the long haul, left to my own devices. I gave up seeking treatment from him when, as a last resort, he prescribed a drug they use for epilepsy, at half strength, to 'distract my brain' from the pain, to use his expert language.

I had been working on one too many TV shows and got to know, firsthand, what 'burn-out' means. I had been promised work until Christmas but, on the Friday afternoon before Thanksgiving I was called into the Executive Producer's office and told that it was my last day. They told each of us late in the day, so we didn't walk off the job a half-day early. That way they could forgo forking out on the payroll for the two-day holiday during Thanksgiving week. They had driven us overtime, getting enough stories in the can to meet our delivery schedule to the Networks that are broadcasting the show. And they only needed to keep on a skeleton staff to handle post-production. The Network execs flew off to Paris for Thanksgiving. The rest of us hacks were unemployed.

That was late on a Friday. By Tuesday I notice a few painful white blisters on my chest. Small ones, but wow! they hurt like hell if busted. Somehow, I twig that this is shingles, about which I know almost nothing. Trusting soul that I am, on Wednesday morning, with the blisters multiplying alarmingly, I drive down to the famous Santa Monica Homeopathic drug store and asked for their advice.

Wednesday, the day before Thanksgiving proper, everyone heads off to be ready for family reunions, and the city virtually shuts down, so I feel lucky that I can get some quasi-medical attention. No use trying to find a doctor on my medical plan; they've all left town. But why would I need one anyway? Me. Mr Natural, all the way.

One hundred dollars' worth of supplements later I return home from the drug store and start dropping the expensive pills and powders. To no avail. The blisters continue, rampant, and more sections of my upper body, and then the side of my face, are colonised. By Thursday it has run its course unimpeded. I'm in pain and the town is shut. I have to wait until Monday at the earliest to get medical attention.

When the specialist listed in my medical plan for skin complaints gets back from the break, I ask for an immediate emergency consultation at his rooms in Beverly Hills. It's Monday by now. And the intensely painful condition has just got worse, having charged along unimpeded on its merry way, leaving me numb, exhausted. A large section of my chest and shoulder looks like a crocodile skin handbag, before the cleaning and polishing. Extensive, rough scabbing.

As I peel back the shirt that I have draped across my upper body his eyes widen. I can see that he's shocked. I don't want him to be shocked. I want him to fix it. He sends me out of his rooms to consult his medical texts, presumably, and when I return he prescribes antiviral meds (apparently the standard treatment) but he doubts they'll have any effect as they need to be taken with 48 hours of onset or they don't work.

I ask him what he would recommend for 'nerve healing'. He's dumbfounded by my inquiry. Healing? But he's a dermatologist; surely he knows what to do to heal fried nerve endings?

I've looked it up on the Internet; shingles is caused by a resurgence of the virus that caused chicken pox in my childhood. My hardy immune system has held it at bay all that time but under certain circumstances – say you're on meds for cancer and your immune system is knocked out, or just under prolonged stress – the virus opportunistically swarms from its hiding place, or places, in the nerve ganglia … and bingo! You're fried.

He asks, timorously, if my immune system is 'compromised' in any way. 'No, I'm not HIV positive,' I tell him, realising that he's never seen it this bad and has almost no clue how to proceed. He sends me out of the room again while he looks up his reference books, or perhaps he does a search into databases on the Internet; then he calls me back into the room to tell me, basically, he's not any the wiser. He writes me a script for the antiviral medications, saying it's probably too late for them. On my second visit I show him something from the Internet showing that anti-viral meds taken too late can make the pain worse, *which it has indeed done*! He reluctantly extends my sickness exemption to extend some part of the medical plan that I've been paying while working by another week. And he prescribes strong pain meds that he knows, as well as I do, are a virtual invitation to addiction. Some variant of oxycodone.

I'll take anything for relief, but …

The lovely melting effect of the first dose is weaker next time, and I have to double it to get any relief. I know I would have to take more and more, and it doesn't take much reasoning to beware of addiction. So I stop taking them after two days. I really am on my own with this vulnerable body as my prickly habitus.

Three months later I remain suspended in a state of shock from the 24/7 pain. It's not supposed to last this long, is it? I got five weeks' unemployment relief, funded by some tax that either I or my immediate last employer withheld from my salary. That carried me across New Year. Then? Nada. Zero. Zilch. Soon, I will be unable to make the mortgage payments. I don't have a job. The show was not renewed.

Unsettled

After coasting along for twelve years on various TV shows here in southern California my options have dwindled. What can I do? My 'career' – such as it has been, post-ashram days – is what brought me here. I source and produce stories for an assortment of TV shows. Occasionally I draft scripts. That's all I know how to do.

Although I enjoyed my end of the year visits back to Sydney while working for *Beyond 2000*, I hadn't ever thought of moving back to Oz. With an expensively wrangled 'green' card I've worked on other shows for a further six years, and the prospect of Australia has drifted further afield. (I was headhunted for a job based in London, but the offer hasn't eventuated.)

Late January I emerge from my peculiar cocoon and drive up to Oxnard for an event with my Teacher. Sitting listening to him is intense relief, a place to rest my weary nervous system. When I return home, computer games and my meditation practice alternate with upright dozing as I slowly recover.

The question begins to present itself for my consideration: Should I stay here, or should I go back to Oz, with no concrete plan apart from returning to my homeland?

Should I stay, or should I go? It burbles up relentlessly for my attention. Perhaps Australia would be a viable option. But doing what? I don't want to work in TV anymore, and in any case I haven't the money to afford living in the major cities where the shows are made.

Medical care – basic medical care that is – is supposed to be free down under, and I can't afford medicine here in the US because, as I'm unemployed I can no longer afford paying to remain in a managed health plan.

But Australia seems like a backwards move. I start to wonder what else I could do, other than TV production. So the question continues to ring loudly in my brain: Should I stay, or should I go? I really ought to paper the walls with the question, for it plagues me, like a Zen *mondo*. Stay, or go? Stay or go?

I hear that my Teacher will hold a two-day event in Portland, Oregon. I book the cheapest flight I can find, and three nights in a hotel near the event venue.

On the first morning in Portland – it's a Monday – he gives a good-humoured address, ostensibly for newcomers and aspirants. He starts talking about a book someone has given him. He says that he doesn't usually read books, but that he flipped it open at random. It's a book of poems and this line popped out to his attention:

'*You didn't come here to settle down*', is the message. Clear as a bell.

He does a riff about our lives being like overnight stays in a motel. While we're in this temporary accommodation, we're not obliged to redecorate the place. Sooner or later, we have to move on.

You didn't come here to settle down, Victor, just keep on moving.

Again, I hear that he has planned a four-day event at a conference centre in Australia that the Aussie devotees have been developing, in S.E. Queensland. He has selected the name Amaroo from a list of indigenous place names (and partly because one of his sons is named Amar, I guess). They have rescued a rundown property south of Ipswich that was once a pig farm. And squadrons of volunteers immediately started clearing the land, regenerating it with literally thousands of trees, and developed a hillside as a natural amphitheatre.

This has been happening over five years or so, but the events have all been staged at the time known as 'sweeps' in television in the US, where I have been working. That's when the ratings success or failure of a show determine what they can charge stations for programming, so it has been 'all hands on deck' and I have never been able to take time off.

With a favourable exchange rate between the US and Aussie dollars I book a flight to Sydney and a rental car to drive slowly up the coast towards Queensland, dropping in to see friends in various communities on the way. My sister Valerie is house-sitting near Port Macquarie, where she is the ladies' golf champion.

When I arrive at the festival site, I join a trickle of people arriving to stay on the land a day or so before the event proper is to begin. Checking my entry pass at the front gate, a smiling face greets me, saying: 'Welcome home.'

Normally I couldn't tolerate the physical discomforts of camping out. But, there's carpet on the floor of my tent. They must have known I'm in a delicate condition.

After the blissful retreat I return to Los Angeles and dispose of my condo the very next day without even advertising it for sale. Without knowing what I will do when I arrive, I jump. The buyer, a real estate boffin who lives in the same complex, has been waiting for me to vacate. I thought I might have to get in painted, or at least have the carpet shampooed, but he says, 'Don't do a thing, I want to re-decorate myself!'

2

Back in the Land of Oz

Love in taxis

Early September 2001. I fly from Los Angeles into Sydney, where I plan to spend the night (in my friend Brett Wayn's chic apartment near Central), before returning to the airport and continuing on a morning flight to Melbourne. In the cab out to Mascot I get into a conversation with the driver, who is Muslim, and I ask how it has been for him as an immigrant in the so-called 'lucky country'.

He welcomes the inquiry and says he is enjoying living in Australia. (He is very polite and respectful. I hope he isn't just being polite.)

I ask him to teach me how to say *Allah 'u Akbar*.

I can't imagine anything greater than 'God', no matter how variously that ultimate principle is represented in different systems of meaning, and – no problems, human to human – we enjoy chanting the praises together.

Later that morning, when I arrive in Melbourne, I find that my cabbie is also Muslim; I greet him with '*Salaam Alleikum*' and he responds '*Alleikum Salaam*'. I ask him, too, about his time in Australia as an immigrant, hoping that he has been made to feel welcome in his challenging new country and we, too, enjoy chanting: *Allah 'u Akhbar!*

I think he's rather surprised that a mere Aussie could genuinely enjoy such a feeling of solidarity and, as I exit the cab, he asks me: 'Excuse me sir, may I ask: What religion do you follow?'

That could be a hard one to answer. I've hardly ever visited churches, of any stripe. Under my Teacher's guidance I've persevered with a set of daily meditation practices for the past twenty-nine years. I revelled in the discovery that the practices work empirically, regardless of culture, language and religious belief. Hence, I don't feel an allegiance to any one particular form of organised religion over another. The practices I follow work just as well for atheists and believers. They're pragmatic as well as empirical and cut through the walls of separation to connect me with a fundamental level of being, from within.

I find with this understanding as a basic operating platform, I am brought closer to people, and I love hearing the stories of their lives. There's a natural flow of genuine affection available in everyday interactions when I share from the place I've learned to value most highly, among the myriad of secondary attitudes available to draw upon.

So, when he pops *that* question on this Melbourne morning: 'What religion do you follow?' I can't lay claim to any such membership. I wasn't expecting the question, so what pops out of my mouth, without any prior planning?

'Why, the religion of the heart!' I aver. And he gets it.

I get it, too. When people share from the love that is at the root of being, the heart opens, in mutual respect and recognition, and humanity thrives. I make up a motto: 'When you find your way to the heart of love, you'll find no brand names there.'

But even this seems trite in the face of what follows …

A couple of weeks later I'm in Byron Bay. While searching for an affordable house, I'm staying with a dear friend on the south side of town, Rose Fox. My sleep schedule is erratic and I keep waking up in the wrong time zone. As I rely on using Rose's computer to go online, I take the opportunity to check my emails early, before she gets into her working day.

This morning, around 4 am or so, I'm puzzled by a news item from the US that's showing up on the home page. Something about a plane crashing into a skyscraper, in New York. It seems like a publicity blurb for some disaster movie, and I'm inclined to dismiss it as such, but … Wait.

I keep reading.

This is happening *live*.

A plane has crashed into one of the tall towers of the World Trade Center, right near the river in lower Manhattan. What a bizarre accident! I don't suppose anyone would survive a crash like that. And what happens to the people who were in the building?

The story is being updated but there's no definitive report on the details yet. I sneak into Rose's living room and switch on the TV. Morning programming has been supplanted by live coverage from New York and, wide awake, if incredulous, I am watching horrified as another plane crashes into the second tower. *What the fuck is this?*

Rose has lived in the States, too, and soon we're sitting together, watching the news unfold. The internal structures of the buildings start to collapse in on themselves. Is anyone still inside? What's happening to them?

I have loose ends to tie up in LA and a week later I'm back there. By now the authorities are sure this was a calculated, hostile attack. I'd once visited London back when the IRA was bombing letterboxes near Harrods. But this is terrorism in a completely new expression. Hijacking planes and flying them deliberately into civilian centres?

My old friends Greg and George live near the Hollywood Bowl, and that evening they take me to a baseball game at Dodger Stadium. All day I've been impressed by the sight of thousands of cars – it looks like every single vehicle in the typical flow of traffic – all sporting a flag; the Stars and Stripes, everywhere I look. Among the disparate ethnicities that populate this city I've never felt such a feeling of pulling together like this. Instead of sniping at each other across the racial divides, the shocking events over East have re-awoken a sense of national pride all over the country and the populace is proud, and defiant!

Nowhere is this truer than in the baseball stadium. People are still not sure if further attacks might be imminent, but they are coming out *en masse*, to a public event – itself a potential target, surely – using the national game to celebrate their pride in the home of the brave and the land of the free.

Bold lighting throws the action into high relief; the players seem larger than life (we have seats right on the fence line, and these men are athletes, built to scale!) On the pitch, the vivid green of the grass could have been painted on for a movie shoot and, spot-lit proudly above the scene, the largest flag I've ever seen ripples massive in the breeze, as every throat roars the nation's anthem.

Today, I am attending a ceremony to take up the opportunity to gain dual citizenship, a possibility that the government back in Australia has just legislated to allow. Half of my family tree, on my mother's side, is rooted in America, so I've come full circle. I've been coming here since 1973, and lived and worked here, this time, for nigh on thirteen years.

Now, just a few months after the horrific attacks on the World Trade Center, I've joined with three thousand other 'resident aliens' gathering to take the oath of allegiance here in Los Angeles. This is just one of two such ceremonies to be held in this city today, with who knows how many others scheduled in other locations.

Despite its position as a world power and a historical record of paranoia towards certain other countries, today the great United States is showing its generous, heart-welcoming side. (A side that I have had personal experience of, through my darling Yankee Grandma.)

The judge who administers the Oath of allegiance tells us his personal story: His father escaped Nazi Germany and entered the country with nothing but 'a suitcase full of books and five dollars in his pocket'. Here, just one generation later, his son presiding as a judge. His personal testimony makes my heart swell. But it's not all schmaltz, there are moments of laughter too. Such as when he goes through the list of countries represented by people in this ceremony and asks them to stand as he goes through the list.

He mentions Austria (and no-one stands). I keep waiting to hear 'Australia' but before long, when it becomes obvious that he is working through his list in alphabetical order, I suppress a wry grin that they often don't know the difference. Homegrown Americans often express surprise: 'You speak good English for an Austrian!' (Most visiting Australians will give you anecdotes like this.)

The funniest moment is when the judge gets to Mexico on the list and a huge majority of the attendees stand. They, and everybody else, break into laughter.

When I had my final interview last year (after the fingerprinting, the FBI check, etc.), I had to go downtown to the Federal building that houses the LA branch of the Immigration Department (US Citizenship and Immigration Services, or USCIS). I had studied the questions they might ask, to check what I knew of the history of this great country. As a result of my study, I can recite the first thirteen colonies (although I was not surprised that none of my American friends could do so). I also had to take a test to ascertain whether I could speak the language. (The official doing this final vetting of me was from Nigeria!) Downstairs, the line of people queueing to apply for permanent residence ran all the way down the street and around the entire city block that this very large building occupies.

Need I say more? It's a complex country, and there are many internal contradictions. But I recognise a warmth gleaming through the rubble and I remember that feeling from that darling Yankee grammaw, who emigrated to Fremantle so many years ago, and the love and generosity she generated within her sphere of influence in a new country, a world away.

Welcome home!

Early 2002

East coast Australia. The inimitable Rose Fox is driving me around Byron Shire, showing me the various areas that I might consider as potential places to live, *pro tem*. Given my peripatetic history, it would be a comfort to settle!

In contrast with the dry landscapes of southern California to which I've become accustomed, here there is bushland; there are farms, and an abundance of lush green foliage on all sides. The green is a cooling (and invigorating) balm to my vision.

Then there is the presence of the ocean, the Pacific Ocean in fact, stretching all the way up the east coast and further. Across the dunes from Rose's house I come across an almost deserted beach, part of Tallow Beach that stretches for some seven kilometres. I'm sitting on a dune, wondering what direction my life will move from here and feeling more than a little flat, when I notice a couple of whales working their way north, breaching from time to time and languidly flopping back into the waves. They don't appear to be traveling with a pod, but from my position I can't really tell. They certainly seem to be enjoying themselves, which lifts my mood somewhat.

I notice a difference in colour between them. Is it an effect of the light? When the tails flash in the sunlight, one of them appears to be silver or white, rather than black. That's odd.

It will be a while before I understand that this was not just some optical illusion.

After scoping out the housing options, with my sister's agreement I zero in on a house in Ocean Shores, in the north of the Shire. I've lured Val up from Port Macquarie (where she is the current Ladies Golf Champion), with the promise of a more challenging championship course, with its own interesting development history (involving prominent figures as entrepreneurs, running the gamut from Pat Boone to Alan Bond!)

A small voice inside wonders why it's the cheapest house in all of Ocean Shores. I remember to ask the real estate agent if it has ever flooded. Apparently, the water from the 'lake' came up to the back steps in the famous Mother's Day floods, back in 1987, but the house is 'considered safe at 100-year flood levels'. Safe or not, we take out an insurance policy which includes flood damage.

It has four bedrooms and three bathrooms (two of them ensuite!) and it's about a mile from the ocean (after 13 years in California, I've all but forgotten thinking in kilometres). The unfenced yard backs onto a small lake (more an over-large pond) on our side of 'Waterlily Park', as it's called – and the bird life is endlessly fascinating. And 'water dragons' scurry through the underbrush, reminding me of the more colourful iguanas in the US. They range widely in size and there's one very large granddaddy (or mummy) that doesn't bother scurrying anywhere. It seems to have been around forever and spends most of its time parked on the upstanding branch of a half-submerged tree in the lake.

I enlist the aid of a local builder, Chris Brown and an old friend from the ashram days, the artist Tony 'Arno' Lunn, to sketch out a plan for some renovations, and to cover the costs I cash in some dollars from funds invested in a small superannuation scheme.

Victor the hermit crab is changing shells, again. But, after years of living in apartments I begin to feel I could live out the rest of my days here. The house was built on a reclaimed swamp land – 'swamp' goes well with 'Marsh' – a part of the reclaimed wetlands that gave way to a housing development in the 1970s. The house itself is a bit of a disappointment. Built on a concrete slab; it could have come from any typical suburban house anywhere in Australia, in blithe disregard for local climate. Satirically known as a brick 'venereal', the inner walls are plasterboard, and the outer (or veneer) shell is in brick.

'You'll need to render those bricks,' says Tony.

The local trend, I'm told, is to cover up the bricks; if not with concrete rendering, then with a process called 'bagging' (whatever that is). I demur, partly because our funds, even pooled, are relatively limited. Besides, actual bricks – even as a 'veneer' – impress me as a solid option compared to the flimsy apartment construction required back in earthquake country, California. I have become wary of bricks possibly dis-assembling in an earth tremor. Los Angeles always felt a little lightweight; given the regularly revised earthquake codes, updated with information drawn from different quakes and temblors. Buildings never seemed very substantial. Certainly, no-one in his right mind would build in brick over there, and whatever *faux* brick you might see occasionally among the stucco, even in Beverly Hills, is always a façade.

It will take me at least two years to break the habit when visiting others' homes to not go around quietly pushing objects back from the edge … Don't they know? I wonder. Any tremor could send all this stuff flying!

I've transferred the funds from the sale of my West Hollywood condo and inadvertently benefited from the exchange rate. My sister comes up with more capital. At 57, I can draw down a small retirement fund without tax penalties and I use that to pay for renovations. We clear away some of the interior walls to create an open plan kitchen/dining/living area and re-surface the floor with splendid 'floating' timber, in dark river red gum. My brilliant friend Tony Lunn re-designs the space, knocking down a wall here and there, and works at it while I go back to Hollywood to finalise my transition to US citizenship. Somehow, I feel that my time there is not finished, and I do enjoy voting against George W. Bush (albeit to no avail).

Tony and Chris Brown keep working away and, returning from my visit back to LA, I settle in with the renovations almost complete. I drive over a hill to the closest local beach, a very welcome feature in nearby New Brighton. It's late on a Sunday afternoon and I really want to throw myself in the water, especially after thirteen dry years in Los Angeles, where the local Health Department recommended against swimming in Santa Monica Bay.

An anxious thought flickers across my mind: What about sharks? And I hesitate. There are people in the water; they must know the state of affairs here. I think, rather winsomely: 'Oh, I would much rather see dolphins than sharks. But nothing like that ever happens to me …'

I walk cautiously into the water.

At that very moment a pair of those beautiful creatures whizz by me, at great speed, traveling horizontally across the very wave I'm about to enter! Welcome home, indeed.

Some years later, on the television news I see a report from the Gold Coast focusing on a rare albino whale. It has been christened 'Migaloo'. That must be the one I saw from the vantage point of the sand dune behind Rose Fox's house at Tallow Beach. It's like a reminder from an old friend, and it seems that I've found my place, in the right part of the world.

New land, old land

Be watchful …there is a beautiful Grace that appears suddenly … it comes without warning to an open heart – Rumi

I'm sitting in my newly renovated living room in Ocean Shores and the question is pounding at me: 'What do I do now?' I upped roots from Los Angeles without knowing what I could do next. Tracking back, I realise I've been on an almost twenty-year arc working in television production, which I kind of fell into, originally. One thing led to another in apparently random order, and now I'm officially burned out, warding off the incipient flare-ups of 'post herpetic neuralgia' after my gruelling bout of shingles.

I am struck by the feeling that this is one of those moments when life gives you the chance to dream: If I had my 'druthers', what would I like to do for the rest of my life? (Or at least, get involved with, next?) Whatever presents itself, given my past history, the next of these choices could lead any-bloody-where. The Centre lies within. That might sound glib, but it is true for me.

If there were no other issues to consider (like income, for example, or any other practical necessities) what would I really like to do?

I come to my own conclusion; all by myself: I would really like to take this book seriously. Give it a fair dinkum chance to come out of its hiding place and tell me what it's really trying to be!

This is the manuscript I've been calling *The Boy in the Yellow Dress*, following my encounter with Henrietta Bernstein back in Cathay Circle, LA. Instead of working at it only sporadically, why not give it a real shot? Take it and find out where it wants to go. Concentrate on that as my first priority, rather than trying to squeeze it into down-time between more pressing gigs.

But how?

That's when things really swing into gear, as if 'the Universe' (a term much in vogue in these parts) has been waiting for a conscious intention to emerge before the next act of the play gets underway. Time to stop rehearsing. I'm already on stage, and people are waiting … It reminds me of that brief moment in time in Sydney, when I extricated myself from the clutches of the wannabe 'de-programmers' and found my way back to my true path.

Recently I joined the local writers' centre in Byron Bay, and was delighted to discover their annual writers' festival, which I have just attended. They are offering a workshop on writing memoir and to my delight the opportunity immediately assuages all sense of loss, of quitting my struggling career, leaving the big smoke and settling by the sea.

'You should check out the Uni. of Queensland', suggests the workshop facilitator. 'Amanda Lohrey is there at the moment …'

Now there's a name to conjure with.

On the way back through Sydney I picked up two books recommended by the staff of a bookshop in George Street. One of them – about the White Australia immigration policy, as it was operated in the early pearl-diving history of Broome, W.A. – has been written by a chap who lives here in Ocean Shores; John Bailey: *The White Pearl Divers of Broome*. Broome. That's in West Australia, but it's the part of the state I have never visited. Coincidentally, I live in Ocean Shores and Bailey does, too.

The other book recommended by the staff in the bookshop, Camille's Bread, is written by the same Amanda Lohrey recommended by the facilitator in the memoir-writing workshop.

The next weekend, there's a small notice in a national newspaper inviting applications for a Master's program in creative writing at … guess where? Yes, none other. The University of Queensland. I make inquiries about joining this creative writing program up in Brisbane. It's not really close to Ocean Shores, but Southern Cross University in Lismore, while closer than Brisbane, has been a little less than welcoming, wanting me to pay fees to do undergrad writing subjects before thinking of a higher degree in writing. A series of apparent coincidences continue to point me towards Brisbane, where a research degree is a no-fee degree! (Queensland styles itself as 'the smart state'!)

Now I think about it, there was that psychic reading I had when my friend Susan Peters and I went searching out a Psychic Faire, in Long Beach, California during my brief return to LA. The psychic told me that where I was living was not where I would be 'working', that I would have to travel north to do research.

Events begin to accelerate. I find that I also need to research and write up a theoretical paper to accompany the creative work; an 'exegesis'. I ring the person in charge of admissions for this course, to ask for advice on how one writes up such a proposal. I speak with Amanda Lohrey.'

'Mr Marsh,' she advises, 'We tend to find that if someone can manage writing up a proposal, they can usually hack the program itself.'

Entry to the writing program is competitive, and the number of places is limited. But I don't shrink back.

I haven't been at university for 35 years – i.e. if you don't count a smattering of some evening classes at UCLA (Spanish language and broadcast journalism), and the two years part-time at the Institute for Gay and Lesbian Education in West Hollywood. But it's been a long time since my honours degree in Perth in the 1960s. How do I make up for a gap measured in decades?

Stuff it! I think to myself. I'm not planning to get just another piece of paper, some qualification for a late-life career change; as if anyone would want to employ a nearly 60-year-old, burned-out shit-worker from TV! But I do know what I want to write about. And what I will need to research. I have two days to put together an application.

But I wonder where is the theory that would give support to my exegesis?

If thoughts register with a degree of intensity in mental space, this one is really loud in my head and, as I walk out of my bedroom, through the archway into the living room, I pass the built-in bookcase that my friend Andy Laycock has constructed for me along the back wall. I'm totally focused on this question: Where will I find the theory for this project?

A book comes flying off the shelf and lands abruptly on the floor.

I'm not kidding. This cannot be ignored. An odd event in 'real world' space responding, in a curious way to a mental event. Curiouser and curiouser!

It's titled *Memories, Dreams, Reflections: an autobiography* by Carl Jung. Here he is again! I'm writing memoir, or autobiography. I spent some earnest time delving into Jung's discoveries during my time at IGLE in West Hollywood.

A stream of synchronous events seems to be guiding me. Don't resist Victor!

A motto in Latin is carved into the lintel over the doorway to Jung's house in Küsnacht – *Vocatus atque non vocatus deus aderit* – and it also appears on the gravestone marking his burial place: 'Whether invoked or not invoked, the god will be present.' But is that God with the capitalised 'G', and why does this man interest me so, given that I have tried so conscientiously to mark out a different path into the great mystery than through the Judaeo-Christian traditions?

Jung came from a lineage of Lutheran pastors, but one of the most striking images recounted in his autobiography was when, at a young age he was undergoing some kind of nervous crisis, he had a vision of God shitting on the spire of the main cathedral in his city.

Young Jung was spooked and resisted the threat of such a blasphemous vision; but it marked the way to free him ultimately from accepting standard received conventions. Jung wrote: 'I can understand myself only in the light of inner happenings. It is these that make up the singularity of my life …'

In his *Modern Man in Search of a Soul* he re-states what appears elsewhere in his writings:

> I have treated many hundreds of patients. Among those in the second half of life – that is to say, over 35 – there has not been one whose problem in the last resort was not that of finding a religious outlook on life. It is safe to say that every one of them fell ill because he had lost that which the living religions of every age have given their followers, and none of them has really been healed who did not regain his religious outlook. [Jung, *CW*, vol 11, ch 11, p. 22]

I know what I want to write, and I know now what I want to research. The story of the dress – the sissy boy in Perth survives the 1950s – is already well underway. And I don't want to focus on HIV/AIDS; on death and dying. Must that be the inevitable outcome for someone so out of step with conventional mores, as I have been?

My survival has been as a direct result of meeting up with my spiritual Master, my Teacher Prem Rawat, and putting into practice what he has recommended for me over many years. It's been a totally pragmatic aid to my journeying to this point and it's tried and tested through lived experience. As far as I am concerned, he's the real deal. Mine is the story of a notoriously 'gay' man who has turned to 'spirituality' even when the prevailing, religious view of people of my alleged 'type' is hostile (even behind the sometimes-condescending smiles).

Is this worth drawing to the attention of a reader? I don't know, but I'm starting to feel justified to give it some serious attention.

Despite the toxic teachings of conventional churches, is it just possible that some of us who don't fit neatly into societal norms might be actually *blessed*, spiritually, as we go about answering our most pressing questions? A convergence of coincidences – more real-life experience of *synchronicity* (thank you Doctor Jung!) – is urging me to stop apologising for my so-called 'queer' nature and take my own life seriously; all of it, including not only my loosely called 'sexual preference' but what I can only loosely call my 'spirituality'. These terms are all so wonky. So is 'self-respect' – what a cliché! – but it has been a vitalising re-growth from out of the baffling aftermath of shaming, in practical terms.

Thus begins, or continues, a thoughtful re-assessment of my journey so far, a process seeded with my studies at IGLE. When a lot of coincidences occur like this recent, fresh sequence, the bells start ringing and I know I'm onto a good track.

I remember watching a doco series on PBS back in 1986 that was hosted by Bill Moyers, which featured the Jungian-inspired teaching of Joseph Campbell, who often spoke about the importance of *following one's bliss*; in other words, of being in accord with one's deepest needs for fulfilment and happiness.

Asked by Moyers during the interviews whether he had ever had the sense, when 'following his bliss', of 'being helped by hidden hands', Joseph Campbell replied:

> All the time. It is miraculous. I even have a superstition that has grown on me as a result of invisible hands coming all the time –

namely, that if you do follow your bliss *you put yourself on a kind of track that has been there all the while, waiting for you*, and the life that you ought to be living is the one you are living. When you can see that, you begin to meet people who are in the field of your bliss, and they open the doors to you. I say, follow your bliss and don't be afraid, and doors will open where you didn't know they were going to be. [Campbell. 120. Emphasis added]

So, for my research project I decide that I will investigate autobiographies by gay men that have a 'spiritual focus'. How perverse can you get? Perhaps I really should title my book 'A Compendium of Blasphemous Transgressions'.

I've recently read one of Christopher Isherwood's last books, about his 40-year association with an Indian guru in Hollywood California, titled *My Guru and His Disciple*. (The Temple where he worshipped is just a few blocks from my first apartment in Hollywood, although I will not visit it until later in 2005 to do some interviews when researching my dissertation.)

Spiritual autobiographies by 'gay' men – how provocative! That might just be an original area for research. How many of those would there be? So, I mention the Isherwood in my research plan.

I also insist on writing against the grain that has been dominating the current view of queer folk; namely the shocking impact of disease, of HIV and AIDS, of death and dying, which plays so predictably into ignorant, neo-religious prejudice. I want to trace the importance of pathways of growth rather than the damnations produced by ideologies based upon the tortured imaginations of binary religions. I am troubled by the gendered representation of he-man 'God' in these ideologies.

As a student of a non-dualistic (Advaita) Vedanta tradition, Christopher Isherwood described this Hindu tradition (as he encountered it under the guidance of his wise and well-seasoned guru, Swami Prabhavananda), as a religion which recognises the male-female principle within the Godhead. 'The Hindu, believing that the Godhead must, by definition, embody all possible functions, is logically brought to think of it as being both male and female.' And he continues, 'One of the greatest causes of misunderstanding of Hinduism by foreign scholars is perhaps a subconsciously respected tradition that God must be one sex only, or at least only one sex at a time.' [Isherwood. Ch. 3]

I feel I have struck paydirt as soon as I venture beyond the limited conventions of the Christian moralists. I feel that my life is unfolding like a scroll ... and that I am deciphering it by writing it.

Meanwhile, I go up to Amaroo to see my Teacher Prem and unexpectedly encounter him in the courtyard of Daya's restaurant. He asks me how I am doing and, a little shocked that he remembers me (it has been a while!), I tell him I've returned to live in Australia,

'Duh!' is his wry response. (As if he doesn't know that!) I recover my wits and tell him I've been doing a bit of writing. Coincidentally, the evening before, in precisely the same location, someone has been pestering him to read their poems.

'Just what you need; another Aussie writing,' I say, almost nudging him in the ribs. But he stops me in full flight, saying, with his finger raised to emphasise the point: 'No, we need that, too!'

When I get back from Amaroo I find that my hastily put together application to join the writing program at the university has been accepted. It turns out that Amanda Lohrey is interested in Isherwood too as one of what she calls 'the Hollywood Vedantists' and has read this very book I have decided to use as a lens to focus my research. Namely, this much-neglected and seldom-respected late autobiography, *My Guru and His Disciple*. An 'out' gay man, who studied under a guru who did not reject him on the basis of his 'sexual orientation'?

'Are you going to do this part-time, or full-time?' she asks me.

I'm still feeling burnt-out from nearly twenty years in television work and, knowing that I would have to settle in one of the major cities to get back into TV, my residual post-shingles neuralgia starts to niggle, and I instinctively reject that possibility. There's a clear signpost for me: 'Don't go down that road again!' I have made only fitful progress on the autobiography, squeezed as it always has been after hours, and in between jobs. I really want to focus on this project.

'Full-time!'

'How are you going to support yourself? Have you applied for any of the scholarships?'

Surely they don't give student scholarships to people my age?

'Well, apply for them all anyway' she advises, 'and we'll see how that turns out.'

Deluge

June 2005. I'm 60. I'm working towards what has now become a full-on PhD at the university in St. Lucia, but I am always happy to return to my home base, in the quiet end of Byron Shire. Valerie has moved on to live with her new paramour, Judy, who is enjoying the liberating effects of loving another woman, after three 'conventional' marriages. Lady golfers at her club may cluck a disapproving chorus from the sidelines but Val powers on, winning the local championship again and again and earning some grudging respect, even as an avowed lesbian.

And the scholarship came through. They actually support my research program at the Uni, and they bumped me into the Doctoral program. I've been beavering away for some time.

I have arranged to meet my thesis advisor in Brisbane, Ruth Blair, who will soon retire after heading up American Lit. studies at the Queensland Uni. I am lucky to have her attentions as I try to wrap up the final draft of my dissertation. Again, another meeting with a remarkable woman, she gets what I'm on about, sometimes more clearly than I do, and I am fortunate to gain her attention after a couple of false starts with other thesis advisors; some of them have baulked at any mention of 'spirituality'. (And I understand why they would, in this bastion of intellectual reason.) From the sidelines, Amanda Lohrey alerts me: 'You'll have no trouble writing about 'queer' and 'gay', but you'll have to seek out another language to discuss spirituality.')

There's a large exhibition of Buddhist icons advertised for public display at the Brisbane Town Hall, and Ruth and I intend to check that out before taking refreshment in a charming teahouse in a central city arcade nearby. We meet up at the civic square outside the exhibit but, just before entering the gallery, I get a phone call from my sister Val, back at home base in Ocean Shores. Val is alarmed that the previous few days' heavy rain has now reached flood proportions.

She and her partner Judy are doing their best to staunch the back doorway, to prevent the flood waters penetrating our home, and they are busy trying to lift as much as they can, up onto higher surfaces. Water is backing up from all the drains, and the three toilets, into the house, and the overflow from the aged swimming pool has covered the front yard and entered the garage.

The roads back south through the Gold Coast are being cut off by floodwaters.

I am virtually trapped in Brisbane, with no option but to wait it out. I try to put my worries on hold, and Ruth and I decide that we might as well go into the exhibition as planned. While I am perturbed by the news from down south, my concerns are tempered by the helpless feeling that there's simply nothing I can do about the situation at the present time.

I make sure that Val and Judy are safe, and Ruth and I go into the exhibition.

An enterprising and kind man who teaches Pali, Sanskrit and early Buddhist texts at my university, Primoz Pecenko, has prevailed upon the School of Religion, Philosophy and Classics to take Buddhism more seriously. As a side bar, he has organised for a collection of icons to be loaned by assorted citizens and institutions from all over Brisbane and its suburbs, which form the bulk of the display.

Once inside, I am stunned.

To all sides, wherever I look, the serene face of the Enlightened One is re-iterated, countless times, in a dizzying array of forms, ranging from tiny miniatures to large statues, all in different media: sculptures, carvings, formal tankas and other paintings; representations drawn from many different cultural and ethnic styles of this great religion.

I am spinning in a hall of mirrors, every image reflecting the same impassive face ... the level gaze of equanimity, neither nor rejecting, inwardly focused. I am surrounded by myriad reminders of my own Teacher's mysterious benevolence, as though the entire exhibit has been arranged to catch me, just as an incipient personal crisis is about to unfold.

In the coming months I will get a deeper sense of what 'equanimity' entails, and just how it might benefit me in practice, from day to day.

After taking time out for tea, I go back to the house in Auchenflower, where I am staying overnight in the house of friends who are temporarily out of town.

What can I do but meditate? It might not seem like the most practical response, but to obsessively check the weather reports and the road conditions further south always brings the same news (and invites the same anxiety), so I surrender to the inevitable, and try to recuperate where I know the source of peace resides, inside, with my ever-patient Teacher. I remember how Brisbane itself had been flooded in 1974 and how well our two ashrams had been protected.

As I close my eyes, His face is there, on all sides, wrapping me in reassuring comfort, silently reinforcing the message.

Next morning before checking out TV weather reports, I meditate again. The floodwaters have begun to recede enough to open the highway, so I drive south, careful to avoid the pools that still flank the flattest sections of roadway. Val and Jude have managed to lift some stuff up and away from damage, but the influx of water has been inexorable. Plasterboard walls have soaked up a foot of dirty water, there's mud all over the glorious redgum flooring and the carpets in the hallway and every bedroom are sodden. These will all have to be torn up, a tiresome task that will require physical strength and a level of perseverance that I couldn't, under normal circumstances, willingly muster. I get to work on ripping up the carpet and underfelt and start to drag it all out to the front kerb.

Out front, emergency vehicles drive through the flooded roadway and the bow waves from their passing shake the garage door off its tracks, disturbing the ducks that have taken refuge within. The standing hot water storage tank is flooded. No electricity is yet available to check if the major appliances have been affected. Food threatens to go off in the old fridge.

When I write that 'all the floor coverings' must be lifted I should point out that means that everything sitting on the floors, including built-ins, furniture, beds, shelving units, etc., need to be lifted and relocated elsewhere for the time being. The 'floating' timber floor does literally that, much to our wry amusement, if not to the beak of the visiting insurance assessor who confesses: 'That will have to be replaced', thereby committing herself and the company to a rather expensive reparation.

The foam underlay over which the flooring was originally laid – all ninety-three square metres of it – has already begun to pong as the water and the mud are ebbing away, leaving a residue of mud and grit. The antique swimming pool in the front yard now hosts a quantity of tiny fish that have found their way in from the lake out back and the pool has sprung a mysterious leak or two. Water from the exceptional rainfall have flooded the waterways of the golf course across the road. We're directly across from the eighth tee.

My old friend David Lovejoy, who founded the local community newspaper, and knows a lot about local politics, tells me that whenever the developers – who have repeatedly challenged local regulations restricting building permits for new areas – have applied to the local Shire council and been knocked back, they have appealed to some Land Court in Sydney. Under State rather than local council law, they developers have always won.

The flood plain of the river has been blocked by newer housing in places like Fern Beach. Consequently, the north arm of the Brunswick River (known as Marshalls Creek), has backed up into the golf course and crossed the road to meet up, through all my living areas, with the advancing waters of Waterlily Park's wee lake. In my back yard.

The pile of detritus on the front verge grows by the day.

The aging swimming pool never regains its previous functional status, and parts of the brick fencing wall at the front and side of the house have cracked and subsided. A section of wooden palings (in Perth we would call them pickets) has given way entirely, betraying their advanced age, and now hang uneasily off their once upright corner posts.

Bob Carr, the gormless State Premier, flies over the area in a helicopter, glibly pronouncing it a disaster zone, before flying back to his office in Macquarie Street. His pronouncement has little effect in alleviating our inconsequential inconvenience, for any calls for emergency assistance tend to remain unfulfilled as soon as we admit to being 'insured'.

But I want this fixed! It's more than a distraction; it is becoming an ever-present disruption of my time. I'm living on cold, wet concrete floors. No matter how urgently I want to return to 'normal', everything takes so much longer than the mere exercise of willpower might desire, so my usual bull-at-a-gate haste with physical tasks simply doesn't cut it.

While I hear virtually nothing from locals, I am not facing the tedious task entirely alone. Occasional bursts of assistance come from unexpected quarters, to my grateful, tearful surprise. Howard Rowe, a kind and gentle builder whom I barely know, turns up with his resourceful toolkit and almost single-handedly takes up the timber flooring. Sections where furniture has been built over the floor are really troublesome, but Howard is relentless and goes at it like a determined ferret.

I want to have him bill me, so I can pass that on to the insurance company, but he won't hear of it. He passes off his two days of serious physical work as 'lending a hand'.

And then Andrew Lohrey, the husband of my thesis advisor, loads some tools in his car and drives down from Brisbane to lend a hand, too. I have an unexpectedly happy time re-building the drooping section of side fencing with him. I have never realised before how crafty men can have such fun in hardware stores! Andrew's calm demeanour (Andrew meditates too) helps me to side-step resentment and shows me that this situation is at least potentially re-solvable, even now, when it all seems too damned hard.

The insurance company keeps ringing me to arrange a time for a clean-up crew to remove the sodden flooring, ignoring my repeated reports that we have taken care of that already, without their assistance, in the first few days. As the weeks and months pass, communication with the assessor develops into a tiresome tussle, with her trying to fob me off with cheaper alternatives for expensive jobs such as the flooring.

I can't just book tradies to take on the work. The insurance company needs to approve the quotes submitted. I must coax and cajole tradesmen to come out simply to provide quotations for jobs, sometimes two or three times over, at the assessor's insistence. These young men are swamped with work, already reluctant, and hard to wrangle. Even when I get the assessor to actually green light a job, it can take weeks to actually attract the appropriate tradies to the site. With several jobs on the go at any one time, there's no commitment from their side as to starting dates, let alone finishing those jobs to which they may or might not have committed.

And for these young guys, there's always the lure of the surf.

I am being stretched beyond patience. I was never particularly interested in mechanical tasks and, as a kind of seven-days-per-week project manager, I am working at the limits not only of my limited technical competence but of my motivating interest in the task.

Months into the job, friends innocently ask what I've been up to and, when I mention I'm engaged with renovations necessitated by the flooding, they are bemused: 'Wasn't that some months back?' they say. I grind my teeth and try to keep smiling.

Every day my resentment threatens to turn into outright anger, and that threat continues, week after week, for many months. *I don't want to be dealing with any of this!* It's not my fault, etc., etc. But I've been forced into a corner. None of my previous experience has provided me with the skill sets required, but dammit! I must respond. I simply must deal with this, whether I want to, or not.

Unless I maintain my equanimity, everything grinds to a halt. I am forced to recognise, and quickly, too, that the opportunity for anger – nay, rage! – doesn't do anything for my clarity of mind. The visit with those Buddha images come to me again and again. Still living on damp concrete, moving furniture from one room to another in rotation, meditation is the only path to clarity, and I must accede to the superior principle of equanimity as central to my daily practice, across the days and weeks and months …

At the most pragmatic level, frustration simply doesn't work, and rather than feeding my deep resentment, or losing my temper, or expressing dissatisfaction, or grumbling at my lot, I am forced to come up with a rather different response more adequate to this pressing task – albeit one that I have not chosen – because unless I can maintain a clear head I will not see problems looming before they crash down on my head. Certainly, anger does not entice the tradespeople (they have plenty of work), let alone the insurance assessor, to become more cooperative.

So, against all my normal inclinations I must practice this interminable series of physical and management tasks as a discipline, as a kind of spiritual discipline, nonetheless, which is probably a good thing. Who knew that the zone of work could function as fundamental, if gruelling, training in managing one's own mind? If I 'lose it', I lose. If I spit the proverbial dummy and do nothing, nothing progresses. I need a clear mind … or frustration and misery are the certain result.

A year to the day after the flood, the final project (replacing the front fence) is complete, and I have – for the second time now – a renovated house. Thereafter, each time the rains come I will nervously gauge the progress of sheets of water as they spread across the back garden towards the house. The so-called one-hundred-year flood plan is now revised down to a mere fifty-year 'plan'.

Looking back, I realise that I have seldom taken on something that requires long-term commitment, when it has not been something for which I am temperamentally suited. TV work was going to a job, and I kept running with the treadmill. Pursuing the research interests for the degree, on the other hand, has been a relatively pleasurable task. I've spent months in a virtual dream state following up every lead prompted by my research interests, but the effort to sustain the argument of a slowly emerging thesis – all mental work – has been lethargic, to say the least, even a tad self-indulgent.

Now I find, to my amazement, that with the countless interruptions that come from acting as a *de facto* building and renovation manager it has all provided a physical and pragmatic pathway that has stretched my patience and my interest in completing something unpleasant, long-term. During the year that it has taken to complete the renovations, I get more work done on the dissertation than I have in the previous two years, working at my own, easily distracted pace.

A different kind of strength

As for the 'mental work', that continues apace at the university where I am allowed to investigate and strengthen my polemic for a different understanding of what it means to be here, now, as a marginalised person ... This is an extraordinary time!

I relish the opportunity to pursue different lines of research and I get the chance to present papers at occasional academic conferences in my field. It's a good way of testing my thinking and I sometimes re-write the papers in a different more formal style before submitting them as essays to academic journals. It's hard to believe, but the University gains research points from the Federal government from my little achievements. I can try out my developing polemic through the rigorous assessment of peer reviewing that each one goes through to be accepted for publication. These various styles of writing are excellent training in writing in different registers, or 'voices'.

I believe the queer interrogation of heteronormativity is a project still in process, with important implications into the future. I propose that a new understanding of the possibility of a queer spirituality (and a pragmatic one at that) will emerge to carry that interrogation beyond the struggle for civil rights, marriage equality and so on, as important as these have been as litmus tests for 'liberation', at the social, political, philosophical and legal level.

Homophobia has many and varied effects, but to drive shame deep into the developing psyche is to dislocate the subject and impair the sense of selfhood, at the bud. Where there is harm, healing is necessary. Personal injury to the sense of self may produce psychological and emotional harm, but the effects are ontological as well as psychological. 'Ontology' is the branch of metaphysics dealing with the nature of being. So apparently 'theoretical' analysis gives me some perspective on what constitutes being and identity within a wider frame than the humdrum, street level that I live within, and will have an acute bearing on my search for capital 'M' Meaning. Where do I fit in this world? And do I need to 'fit'?

Whether it is driven by religion or psychology, with its quasi-scientific status lending it authority in the Age of Reason, the homophobic constructions that seem to apply to me are always toxic. To be 'gay' (or 'queer', which is my preferred term) is represented as a psychopathology. I begin to recognise the status of powerful 'God' figures as 'representations' rather than immutable Creator figures and find that both Michel Foucault (in *The History of Sexuality, volume 1*) and Hanna Arendt (in *The Human Condition*), help me understand the powerful link between 'control of divine forgiveness and control of society'. This is a breakthrough insight for me.

My favourite commentator of comparative religion, Alan Watts, did so much to build bridges across religious differences, taking up training as an Anglican priest (in this setting, the Episcopalian version) as well as studying the practical and theoretical ways of Zen Buddhism. Watts pointed to the nexus between the spiritual and the social in the Judaeo-Christian tradition, which 'identifies the Absolute – God – with the moral and logical order of convention'.

Watts contrasts this against the 'way' of Zen and describes the conflation as 'a major cultural catastrophe' [Watts. 11]. If Watts's analysis is correct, his corollary is particularly telling for people like me, marginalised by this kind of construction: 'It is one thing to feel oneself in conflict with socially sanctioned conventions, but quite another to feel at odds with the very root and ground of life, with the Absolute itself' [Watts. 11].

I really get my teeth into the resistant counter-narrative by investigating the life and work of Christopher Isherwood, who becomes a kind of 'stalking horse' for raising (and resolving) the issues that fascinate me.

When people ask me what my field of research is, my response – 'spiritual autobiographies by queer men' – produces a range of startled responses, from outright astonishment bordering on disbelief, to (from the more subtle) a wry smile. In any case, the next question will be 'You mean there are such things?' with the not always vocalised subtext: 'There can't be very many of those!' And I am supposed to join in the joke. Of all things that queer men are about, it couldn't be religion, or 'spirituality', the assumption goes. Queer = gay = homosexual = they're all about sex. One later wit announces that heretofore 'the love that dare not speak its name' now won't bloody shut up!

In my early research I am fascinated, then, to find a cache of autobiographical writing by queer men who, despite the common misconception that an authentic religious life could only be pursued if based upon a repudiation of their 'deviant' sexuality, have engaged sincerely with various forms of religious belief and practice.

This rich corpus of texts, narrating spiritual journeys both within and beyond mainstream religious groups, gives voice to experience otherwise silenced by conventional religious narratives.

I get a serious buzz one day when, as part of our training as candidates for research degree, we are given some practical training in research methods, finding out how to use the rich trove of databases available through the well-appointed library at UQ. In the first practice session we look up a database that accesses thesis dissertations in various fields from right across the world and, guess what! There's one that matches my search terms perfectly. In Ohio, of all places, a fellow named Christopher Buren Stewart has been awarded his PhD with a study of 'spiritual autobiographies by queer men'.

I enjoy these subtle nudges of coincidence, for Ohio was the home state of my mother's side of the family. Even better, Stewart has included a major chapter on my chosen case study, Christopher Isherwood, in his dissertation. And guess what? The library will order in a copy of that thesis for my personal perusal.

Isherwood's early life in Europe produced little in the way of spiritual inquiry; it was more an intense experience of disillusionment. Isherwood was more into turning his back on religion and, for a while at least, hoping that the communist experiment in Russia would satisfy his idealism. His restlessness and personal dissatisfaction eventually led him to settle in California, where he was to become famous as a kind of standard-bearer for 'gay liberation', especially after the publication in 1977 of his first 'out' autobiography, *Christopher and His Kind*, which cemented his reputation as an avuncular literary standard-bearer for gay liberation in California.

But something else was going on.

Isherwood, the erstwhile atheist, had 'got religion' after all. But it was not religion in its conventional formation in these here parts. When he and his best friend, the eminent poet WH Auden, emigrated to the US in 1938, declaring themselves to be pacifists on the eve of World War II, Auden stayed on the East Coast, while Christopher headed West.

In Los Angeles he developed a rich network of associates among the European émigrés who had landed in California and he soon gained work as a screenwriter. But one of his intentions in heading to Los Angeles (in addition to pursuing the company of an attractive young man), was to seek out two leading British writers and intellectuals, Aldous Huxley and Gerald Heard, to gain support for his conscientious embrace of pacifism in the time of war. I had read some Huxley in my hippie days, but I hadn't heard of Heard.

Imagine Isherwood's surprise to find these two respected 'role models' seated at the feet of an unusual if not unorthodox spiritual figure, Swami Prabhavananda, a Hindu monk and guru who headed up the Vedanta Society of Southern California and supervised an ashram on North Ivar Avenue, in Hollywood. Here was a whole new way (albeit with ancient roots) of imagining the spiritual quest.

After an initial reluctance to accept a 'God' in any form, Isherwood was persuaded to try some meditation practices, using a mantra and a rosary given to him by these new friends.

Swami Prabhavananda was no soft-headed hippie. Isherwood admired his political awareness, as a former activist in the Indian resistance against British colonialism.

Despite his earlier rebellion, practising a new form of religion caught Isherwood's interest. Disillusioned by the betrayal of its earlier liberal stance on gender equality, his faith in Communism faltered and he was ready to study a system that didn't rely on warmongering.

In California, he settles down to practise his rosary and find ways to serve his spiritual preceptor. He also studied, in some depth, the philosophical principles on which this particular expression of Vedanta was based and worked with Swami Prabhavananda on translations of some of the classics of the Advaita expression of Vedanta.

Reflecting on their work translating the *Bhagavad Gita*, he later writes: 'By the time we had finished ... I realized that I had been studying it with an ideal teacher and in the most thorough manner imaginable.' Just as he had embraced German in the 1930s as a way of rehearsing new possibilities for selfhood, despite his own initial 'prejudice', Isherwood found the 'very Indianness' of Vedanta helpful in the 1940s, when he was exploring new ways to think about his troubled personal history. He was 'grateful to Vedanta for speaking Sanskrit', as he put it. Here he could learn a religion afresh, without the associations carried from the Anglicanism of his upbringing.

I needed a brand-new vocabulary and here it was, with a set of philosophical terms which were exact in meaning, unemotive, untainted by disgusting old associations with 'clergymen's sermons, schoolmasters' pep talks, politicians' patriotic speeches ...'

Isherwood had been tortured by all this cant after his father was killed, near Ypres. At the time he was ten years old and still in boarding school, and he felt pressured most acutely by the jingoistic drumbeating. Not only were the inevitable authority figures beating the drums of war, but his widowed mother, too, joined the chorus.

Isherwood persevered with the practices. His relationship with his guru deepened over decades and he was able to exceed the discursive parameters that should supposedly constitute him, even to himself, as an 'outsider'. The philosophical theory underpinning the sophisticated religion gives his pragmatic meditation practice a refreshing context, especially after the revulsion he felt towards Christianity, in its Imperialist expression.

He tried living in the monastic setting of the ashram in Hollywood but quit it, without quitting the mantra practice, or his ongoing devotion to his guru, and the translation projects that they undertook together. He saw that the goal of spiritual practice is not to destroy the relatively illusory 'false' self – that is needed to function within the changing world of phenomena – but to shift one's centre from close and exclusive identification with it, in order to recover the deepest roots of being within the zone of 'the unchanging' – the eternal, underlying basis of all life and consciousness.

To identify as 'gay' or 'queer' could only ever be a partial view of the self. People who don't understand his 'conversion' experience need to give it a sincere appraisal.

I don't work with these as merely philosophical constructs in my own daily practice, which I take as an entirely pragmatic technique to understand the nature of being; while being me, in my own time, and in this place. But it becomes important in the development of a suitable theoretical basis for my dissertation that I should recognise the strongly unitive, rather than dualistic, basis of this theory that enabled this very original figure to fulfil his *dharma* as a writer and a lover.

As a privileged son of Empire, Isherwood was mocked for accepting teaching from an Indian Swami, a member of an occupied race under British colonial rule, but he learned a great deal from his Swami that the Anglican church had not provided.

It strikes me that the importance of a personal relationship with his teacher deepened over decades. And my own teacher is here now, working with me as I 'wrestle with my angels'; coaching me as I detoxify the stain of shame; learning what it is to be, here, now from the ground up, gleaning meaning from empirical, lived experience rather than from doctrines and theory.

Notes for a journal of awakening

It seems like a perfectly appropriate moment to give myself a Tarot reading, to get another angle on where I am at. I pull The Judgement card – number XX – and it falls in the position for 'Long term' prospects. Should I be scared? What does the reading indicate?

JUDGMENT (XX)

There is long term potential to go way beyond personal limitations you had accepted. *The value you once placed on the outer is being shifted to the inner. You are gaining new capacities for self-knowledge, self-trust and awareness of your divine aspect.* As you allow your petals to unfold, what a bounty of talent, inspiration and visionary ideas are revealed.

Experience has tempered the ego-inflationary potential of this kind of news. But I read on. 'You yourself are an abundant universe – a fertile, creative, blossoming place from which new developments are constantly emerging. Explore this new, exciting, freeing energy of transformation.' (A little encouragement goes a long way ...)

I'm getting nervous. The next card I turn up is in the 'conscience' position and it's the QUEEN OF HEARTS (i.e. Cups), which advises me to 'surrender to the feelings of the heart, your sensitivity and intuition.' And it continues ...

It's as if an inner oracle is preparing to impart a profoundly powerful message to you. Meditate and listen carefully for it. *Whether this is happening because of some stressful situation or accident – or simply because you have reached a level of serenity where your higher faculties are naturally awakening – it truly doesn't matter.* The important thing is that the Queen of Cups represents a heart-connection and *receptivity to higher source*, a look into your world with the eye of Spirit. There is no reason to resist this energy. After such an experience, you see reality quite differently. *Jot down some of your insights. If you process them consciously you will have inspiring material to work with in future weeks and months.*

Paradoxically, at the time when a PhD project is pushing the mental muscle harder than it has been for some time, the call of the intuitive/feeling way of insight has never been stronger. Perhaps the demands of the PhD are to wake me up, so that I am operating in full 'awake' mode.

July 2005

My Teacher Prem has just been talking about tuning the string of your 'instrument': not too tight and not too slack; the range of tension is quite narrow for it to resonate in tune. I think of many occasions where I have been suddenly 'tuned' to a more intense and clearer state of awareness. Occasions that may not have always been pleasant, but the outcome is surprising.

Suddenly you are operating on a new scale of possibilities; you know you are going very fast, vibration-wise, and you had better not trip up on any of your little peccadilloes, or there could be an awful accident, and you could miss the true and lasting harvest of this heightened time.

The body is tugging for attention and a lack of exercise could become a problem if you don't bring the three energies into balance. Shaking off lethargy doesn't seem to be a problem. I am energised, although I do watch too much television.

If this seems to me to be a bogus way of being alone: avoiding people so I can work and introspect. Yet feeding at the communal trough of popular culture for too many hours a day? When I do go out and mingle ('trivia night' – a community event last Sunday) I am very present, quite competitive, and even a bit 'driven'. Perhaps I 'impact' people too strongly, a little disrespectful of boundaries … Apart from the opportunity to gambol in the bliss fields, meditation may also heighten the awareness of my failings!

I notice I am biting away at my fingers like I used to; 'used to' in the days of anxiety. I have always interpreted this as an insecurity gnawing away at myself as I yearn for meaning and significance. Perhaps the attempt to make a stance armed with a PhD – both in the summing up of a life to date and a broader statement of the validity of queer-affirmative subject positions – is forcing me to draw all these issues together and write to draw a line under the whole mess so I can get on with my real life… What comes next?

My 'real life' seems to rely on a greater detachment, born in the floods.

Having resolved the gay thing as an issue at all and welcoming the cooling of the hormonal drive to connect 'out there', finding a solid level of serenity that balances me: it's as if a higher (or is it 'deeper') aspect of being may come in more powerfully to dominate the habit-driven, 'lower' self which has been in control for so long. That foregrounded self has been calling the shots, deciding when to meditate, according to the implicit terms of my agreement with my Teacher, but recent years have built a foundation for what happens now.

How long does a life take to ripen and even bear fruit? Through the practice of this 'Knowledge', as my Teacher terms it (the *Raj Vidya* in Sanskrit), I feel that this joy/serenity/peace and bliss, which is at my core, is the real harvest of a life; yet it is always only a potential unless I go to it. He keeps talking about the oil that needs to be extracted from the peanuts before you cook with it; the butter needs to be churned from the milk, and so on. This is not an automatic process, eh?

But there is a definite changing up of gears happening …

It's high time that I accept that real 'intelligence' seems to be the product of a *heart-felt* wisdom. When the head leads, there is confusion, the familiarities of duality and conflict. When the genital urges take the lead there's a draining of energy and a turning away from the centre. When the heart leads (and it is less assertive than my success-driven 'male' mind) there is insight, even extracted through analysis, and an innate ordering or re-shuffling of merely relative values.

August 2005 Writers Festival time

Am I slowly becoming aware of the energy which supports my growth?

Like the sunlight that gives energy to plants to grow, we are surrounded (we live within) a love field, which is blessing the growth of our 'seed-form' consciousness. Life, in the physical and emotional bodies, is the ground from which our seed consciousness springs, but it is being called forth, if you like, by the sun/love-field energy to grow beyond the conventional boundaries of self-hood.

When the core of our being meets or makes direct contact with that field, really opens to it, there is an experience of intensity, beauty, clarity … and simply, rightness. It is what I am born for. Even the physical and emotional being, that I/we have been, takes second place, or gives way to the primacy of that urge, the inevitability of that goal, the fruition of that life's work.

And to experience it before death comes and snuffs out the opportunity? Is that enlightenment? These days they are more likely to identify this gradual shift as 'awakening'. In the same way that a parent, whose sense of personal goals must give way to a different set of responsibilities to serve the growth of the child, so the physical desires and the selfish emotional wants can be re-directed in maturity, go towards fulfilling the needs of the new child now being born from within.

A new understanding and a new set of priorities is emerging that overrides my old conditioning. To 'give up' sex, to re-integrate the desire for relationship into this potential for inner awakening can then be a willing, joyful surrender, not so much the denial that I have wanted to shy away from. Relationship is less like a search for an intimate partner, and more about recovering an inner connection with the source of being itself. A relationship with another person based on this kind of priority might just mellow pragmatically into wisdom. I've seen living examples of this possibility, even if I haven't yet achieved it myself.

I know that over time, my fuel gets expended, frittered away. So let me use this new inspiration wisely, towards this proper goal from now on, please. Back and forward, progression and regression; it's a painful thing to relapse, to fall back from the 'highs' (or is it the profound depths?) Can I just go forward from now on, instead of falling away? Carl Jung talks about both motions being part of the dynamics of integration; that 'regression' prepares me for a new *pro*gression.

I throw caution to the winds, get out the credit card, start waving it as one magically capable of opening the financial gates required to get me on a plane, and I head off from Brisbane to Kuala Lumpur, to see my wonderful Teacher in person.

Am I being irresponsible?

Sometimes the needs of the heart transcend the laws of finance and logic.

I don't know this at the time, but my dear friend Susan dies in Los Angeles. Not only will she leave me some cash but, in addition, wills her leftover frequent flier miles to me. It's not the first time that I risk taking the step, in faith, and the support shows up later.

On the Malaysia Airlines flight, as we edge towards our destination, a graphic icon of the plane is plotted over a map on the cabin's video screen, and sometimes it shows an arrow pointing from the body of the plane towards … *Makkah*?? Is that Bahasa for North? I wonder. If so, it doesn't seem to be properly aligned.

I switch to watching Spiderman to take my mind off the airline food.

We arrive at KLIA at the crack of dawn and we're whisked into town via empty freeways, past green palm oil plantations backing onto lush tropical rainforest, and we check into a hotel at rates arranged by the local organisers: Prime Academy. Lovely to recognise friendly faces; heart friends in unfamiliar places.

Here in Malaysia, devout Muslims are following the strictures of the holy month of Ramadan. Outside, it is steaming hot and I stay indoors, trying to catch up on some sleep, inevitably compromised by the strictures of travel on a crowded overnight flight. On the ceiling of my hotel room, I notice, is a small brass arrow, pointing … where? To Makkah… oh, that's the direction of *Mecca*, as we would spell it, I realise. For any Muslim traveller ready to make prostration in the direction of the holy place and do the daily prayers, this is a handy orientation: *That way*, it proclaims, silently.

The next day. For around 2,000 people at a conference centre, the coordinates of perfect peace and joy, rather than being in a certain place, are re-located in the moving form of the living Teacher. To my mind, informed by lived experience, he's the Teacher of the Age; the compass point of a lifelong journey for me. So, please indulge me as I open up my story to reveal something of its *transcendental* core …

At a meeting hall prepared in advance, the day opens with a full-on practice session, a valuable reminder at any time of the foundation practices that have steadied me for decades. As we shed the hustle and bustle of getting our bodies to the venue, the vibe in the hall deepens into stillness. Gradually the techniques refocus our minds within … and a profound quietness reigns, inside out and all around. Even the body know this is something special.

We are treated to the full-length, entire DVD of a recent meeting in London, during which my Teacher outlines his plans for his new project, the 'Keys': how newcomers may be brought into the very practical and empirical knowhow/how-to, to engage with the original source, the one with no brand name. We have been calling it the Knowledge; 'self-knowledge' in the manner, perhaps, that Socrates might have used the term (if he spoke English!)

I remember the early days back at University in Perth, where advice from the ancient Greeks was proclaimed, with a bust urging me to 'Seek Wisdom', and the Socratic dictum: 'Know Thyself' carved into limestone along the walkway to the central library. For me, beyond my first degree, this process led me to that small room in Cardigan Street, Carlton, back in 1972, and I was taught how to look within.

'Are you hungry but you're sick of studying recipe books?' was my instructor's challenge (and I *was* very hungry!)

I have resigned from serving as an instructor, after doing that very job for a few years myself. Today, in KL, it is obvious that his plan to make 'Knowledge of the Self' available wherever there is a thirst, and his tireless effort surpasses anything I could ever have imagined. He talks gleefully about how a hypothetical seeker, in the middle of the Saharan desert, will nonetheless be able to download an MP3 file and listen to the talks in which he introduces his teachings afresh! New technologies have never seemed more appropriate, or timely, when they are being used for their highest potential purpose.

After a break for lunch, we watch another, shorter presentation and then Prem, the man himself takes up his rightful position in the chair on the main stage (in front of a leafy image projected as a backdrop).

We have been primed!

It is such a joy to hear him live. His gaze seems to take everyone in, including little me, beaming up from the sixth row. And he beams right back. He seems really happy to see all of us, and expresses his enjoyment at being able to speak to a live audience again, after months of speaking to a 'bloody camera'. (He's been working on the videos for the Keys.)

We have been given a glimpse of the quality of the materials. The short video we have seen included some interview sections with him; and as a former worker in TV, I can tell you, the picture quality is exceptionally fine. I was wondering: has this been shot on film, rather than video? is it the lighting? The colours were so intense and he looked so radiant! He mentions that they were shot on High-Definition video and I am amazed again how he always tweaks his presentations to improve the quality, enlisting the aid of better technology to bring his crucial message to the world, just as he is always tweaking my heart, showing me there is always more to know, and moreover, an ever-deepening field of feeling to explore.

I remember the days when we only had each other's testimonies for inspiration; sometimes leavened by a visit from a visiting instructor, a role I had played myself. We would feel fortunate just to be able to get a copy of an overseas newsletter and we'd read and re-read every tiny section, devouring excerpts from his talks. Otherwise, we had only each other to listen to.

I must have been in a really degraded state considering that after 32 years my heart feels alive today in a way that I can scarcely remember feeling.

How is it that he is always such a surprise? My heart leaps to see him, independently of my petty will; it knows where it belongs (its real home state) even when I am confused and dulled by the business of everyday survival. I am beyond glad that I have made the effort to get myself here.

He likens our hearts to a one-stringed instrument and describes how the Master comes and cleans it, meticulously. The string has been so slack and loose it's been virtually silent. He tightens the string so that it starts to sing and then he gives the instrument back to us, perfectly tuned.

As he says this, he makes a gesture of reaching out, as if giving back the instrument. My own hands go out, instinctively, to receive the gift he is offering from the stage; from his very being, in fact, and I ask him to take my heart and give me a renewed one, perfectly and acutely tuned!

He questions our ability to tell right from wrong. 'You know why it is impossible to know what is good?' he asks. 'Because always, one man's bad is another man's good!' I have been so disappointed at the recent election result, back in Australia, and almost upset to see the PM's glee at his success. One man's good is, indeed, another man's bad!

He gently mocks my tendency: 'You are not Masters, although sometimes you talk like you are one. You are apprentices,' as he gently chides me.

Coming after the Australian election result, which has severely disappointed me, I know that if *that* guy, for whom I have trouble raising more than a baseline of respect, was happy and I wasn't, I was probably identifying with the wrong factors, and I simply had to laugh – it was as though my Teacher knows exactly where I have been – in delusion – and he is encouraging me to come back to a differently ordered reality. That's just 'the way it is', he advises.

His focus tunes my understanding.

For the next 24 hours I swim in an altered state, everything being just 'as it is.' I wonder if I could possibly maintain this state of suspended judgment, seeing the world from a subtly altered perspective, free from all discrimination …

As he talks, there is nothing left of me, just this deep calm. And a heart dancing, unabashed, with him. You can keep all the so-called luxuries of this world … nothing will ever match the sheer enjoyment of this kind of meeting – heart to heart, in synchronised understanding with the King of Hearts. Nothing, that is, until he shows me that there will be more to come in this rare and special kind of enjoyment, with him …

Microphones are standing in place for an 'Expressions' event, where we might get a chance to talk to him. But after our Teacher leaves the stage, the MC announces that he has accepted the request for a greeting line. Soon, the rows of seats are quietly filing out, according to some master plan. Music streams throughout the venue and we are drawn, one by one, towards an entrance where a cloth-lined tunnel leads into a small chamber. And there he is, larger than life, smiling, welcoming me, open-hearted, into his presence. My heart is bubbling with joy to see him so close, and before my head goes to his feet in a sincere gesture of gratitude, his eyes meet mine, affirming that the joy I am feeling is completely real.

From those eyes flows a scintillating stream of love, like an endless source of exquisite precious jewels, dancing, tumbling, intoxicated with the highest forms of laughter, straight into my heart. Love binds us together, and in its essence, it's the true expression of freedom.

I am left babbling this prayer:

> Be the ruler of my heart
> Let me not look to anything else, not even for a second ...
> I don't want to lose the unalloyed joy of finding love with you
>
> I see it in the face of every devotee
> turned to you like flowers to the sun.
> You embody the perfect coordinates of peace
>
> It's no use knowing the coordinates of peace
> without a homing device!
> My heart turns to you and finds its perfect partner.
> I want to dance with you, with eyes only for each other
> and the rest of the world can do ...
> can do ... whatever it thinks is real.
> Meanwhile my heartfelt gratitude flows towards you,
> And I am yours.

I float back into the hall, savouring the joy. After a while, I open my eyes and realise that these large screens on either side of the stage carry projections that now show a live feed of the greeting room, backstage. These images continue throughout the duration of the greeting line. The feeling inside and outside is the same, as we watch the continuous presence of Kindness himself opening his heart to each and every one who comes to him. These moments exist outside of time and will always live in my heart as a precious store of inspiration. Thank you, Prem.

When he was delighting us with his stories, I wanted to store every word, every example, in my memory, but most of the language evaporates. Gathering with other premies over meals in the succeeding hours and days we form our own little islands of happiness amidst the bustle of commercial Kuala Lumpur. Chit-chat has given way to inspiration. I realise that this company I choose to keep is aptly called 'holy' company. The perfect way for human beings to be together and converse, always reminding ourselves what is real, and where joy does reside.

Perhaps it is inappropriate – simply too clumsy – to try to give an account in words of such experiences, but I need to remind myself that such possibilities do occur, and they lift me out of my humdrum expectations and show me a higher/deeper aspect of being, here. And I need to acknowledge and honour these experiences, a transcendental affirmation crowning an enhanced reality, now.

Error of parallax

When I say you are blessed, I mean it! If you haven't found the Divine in you, what is the point in pointing up there? If you cannot see the Divine that resides in your heart, how will you see the Divine that resides in the universe – how?
– Prem Rawat

People often ask me why I still sit in meditation, after all these years. I often cite the example of my son David, a gifted musician and performer, who plays lead guitar and other instruments. I know that he would never play in public if the guitar were out of tune. In fact, he is so clever that he can tune it to different settings, for certain musical styles.

In my early experimentations with guitar, as a teenager, I learned that on the basic acoustic guitar, with its six strings, you tune its strings from the top down to the lowest, which is the slowest to go 'out of tune'. So when I meditate, I use the four techniques I've been taught to return to the 'primordial vibration' of simple being, as I tune up before I go into my day. Otherwise, I am liable to produce discordant responses to whatever situations life serves up to me. If I surrender the thicket of everyday thought sufficiently and achieve a state of attunement in my daily meditation practice, my mind is clearer and freer to respond appropriately.

However, just as the bottom string of a guitar can go out of tune, no matter how well the other strings vibrate in relation to the lowest, unless you have perfect pitch, or an external aid that serves as a tuning fork, you might be producing a sound that doesn't please the ear as you might have hoped, and as the guitar is designed to sound.

Similarly, I can meditate every day using the four techniques, but I might need a tuning from a reliable, external source and that is where the Teacher/Guru/Guide/Coach plays a part in restoring my distracted mind into a better state of understanding.

Another example I use sometimes to explain why I persevere with the practices, is from an elementary lesson I understood from high school physics. Say I'm sitting in the passenger seat and my father is driving and I try to read the speedometer to get an accurate idea of the speed at which we are travelling, I won't get that, because the instruments are designed to be read from the point of view of the driver. I was taught this was called the 'error of parallax'.

So, if I am trying to understand what is happening in my life, I must recognise that there's an alignment necessary so that my brain functions well. Whenever I take the chance to hear from him – and those opportunities take many different forms, not only face to face, but in a changing variety of ways as communication technologies advance – there's an often-subtle shift in my basic understanding of how I understand what living is about.

My Teacher is a Master of changes and he adapts to make use of whatever opportunities these new tools provide him to spread the message and marshal his resources. Sometimes after spending a few days with him I make the wry observation that – at a fundamental level that my rational mind does not quite grasp – my very 'molecules' are being re-arranged or tuned to respond to a higher setting!

Breakthrough (Psyche's wisdom)

Sitting quietly on the floor beside my bed. Through the window the small lake, close to the house, is framed by half a dozen palms and a pair of drooping ficus trees. The scene is populated by an ever-changing population of twittering, squawking, carolling birds. Water dragons, large and small, scurry through the leaves, and the big granddaddy of them all perches on the stark branch of a dead tree that is semi-submerged in the lake. Slowing down, closing my eyes, I allow my attention to be drawn inside.

In recent weeks, my formal meditation practice has ushered me into a new level of peace that has been deepening mysteriously with each sit. At its strongest, it's as though a giant floodgate is being opened inside and a tangle of resistance that I was not previously aware of, is dissolving with the flood.

How much have I fought for focus, for clarity, over how many years? Now the practice of techniques is more about surrendering, of giving way to a deeper level of feeling; learning to receive the experience more than mastering a set of techniques. Meaning has less and less to do with thought.

I've agreed to drive north for the day to join a group of devotees to rehearse a play they are staging to celebrate our Teacher's birthday, but as I give way to the inner release, the priority of that appointment rapidly diminishes. I am a sugar cube dissolving into warm tea, The bonds of Being itself are dissolving in the profound certainty of love.

I often wonder why 'God' figures are projected out and away from us wee creatures. Firmly established now in the profound embrace of peace, it's as though I am being encouraged: 'Rest in the lap of the *Divine Mother*'. This powerful experience is stabilising me from moment to moment and holding me in love, inside. Now deeply settled, I begin to travel.

What? *Travel?* In time ... or space?

In the safety and security of Mother's love I need not resist. I'm sitting by my bed in Ocean Shores. At the same time, I find I am the ten-year-old, sitting alone on my bed, back at the family house in suburban Attadale, in Western Australia, circa 1955. This deeper state of awareness has delivered up a buried memory into consciousness now.

The past unlocks in this timeless present.

I feel how unutterably sad the boy is, to have been so bluntly rejected by his father just now, in the kitchen where his father has been working on re-surfacing the floor. 'You stay out of this', growled his Dad, and his diffident attempt to be like the men roughly rejected, he/I have stumbled back to my room, at the back end of the house, where I sit dumbly with my sense of being safe *dis*-located, and no place to go.

Over the intervening years I have been able to recall that event, but now, for the first time since, it's as though I am being given complete access to inhabit the boy's *feeling* space. I feel the event is crushing me and I put up a flag in my mind so that I will be able to recall this moment, at some hoped-for future time when I will have better resources to deal with the profound shock that overwhelms me.

What is the feeling? The feeling is *desolation*. That's the only word I can find. Beyond oppression – it's flatline, empty … spent.

For five decades he/I must have found ways to 'cope', burying the experience and sealing myself off from its pain.

But now I see that in some corner of my being, I have never fully emerged out of that place – or, only partially; just enough to survive and go on. One copes. All the while I have been offering a cheeky *performance* self, all out on the surface. A self, tap-dancing on the brink of the abyss, deflecting people away from asking me about feeling, rejecting intimacy in order to survive. Otherwise, something threatened to collapse on itself, inside. The broken boy became a guarded, fearful man, biting his nails, smiling nervously all the while. I reject men so I can't be rejected, even while I long to be embraced by them.

Today this mysterious process of recall has brought me back to the very core of a trauma that some innate reflex wisdom has *protected me from* until now, and I am devastated by this feeling of intense desolation. I'm knackered.

I'm two hours late for the play rehearsal and participate only quietly. For several days my energy is scarcely available – flatline you might call it – but eventually it's as though the wound has been utterly cleaned out. It has lost its power over me. Its control has been loosened. I am released, at the root, and now it's just a smooth crater, replaced by a deeper certainty of peace ...

I'm in a state of wonder. I can see how deeply I have needed the strong connection with peace in meditation to prepare me for this spontaneous healing. I mull it over with my dear friend Anne Di Lauro, who is trained as a Jungian therapist, and describes her work as a psychotherapist as helping her clients to locate and strengthen their 'inner healer'.

I wonder about the power of psyche to untangle blocks to a growth that is reaching towards increased awareness from within. You know what it's like trying to untangle a fishing line: you might have to untangle knot after knot after knot until, eventually, you arrive at the original snag that was the root of the tangle.

It seems to me that within the psyche is an ever-present urge for fulfilment. As long as there is this innate force expressing the potential of completion, it will find its way to grow around, over, under blockages, towards the light. And furthermore, it will clear its way, *in its own timing*. This breakthrough has not come about through some formal therapy process. It seems that Psyche knows the way.

If I dawdle in the dumps of depression I can re-run old mind tracks, of course, familiar dialogues with myself and others that might rationalise my standstill, justify my unwillingness to grow. Absurd scripts that I occasionally catch the tail of, as they slip into the dark depths of denial: you're not supposed to have these feelings; and it's okay to throw your life away ... You're not supposed to be here anyway. You're not one of the real people. Your experience does not count. (That's a deadly one!)

Over time I start to recuperate my connection with Frank, my father, *through* 'the wound'; imagining, feeling my way towards, how he must have suffered from the shame of being 'illegitimate', a 'ward of the state', right through his childhood; how lonely he must have felt ... Now I can start to feel empathetically for him. Maybe we share something around a constellation of issues of shame and wounding, inter-generationally; and now I can recognise and applaud his bravery to have made a decent life for himself, and a family, in the world. He had the dignity and the courage to survive and build a life and support a family. I see what those drinking sessions with his buddies after work – for which I had so little respect or understanding when I was young – meant to him.

Another shell has cracked and given way to greater life.

As it deepens over years, I recognise that this breakthrough comes about not as a result of therapy, nor as an outcome of some potency inherent in 'gay liberation', although maybe I shouldn't be so judgemental about the putative gay 'community' that I have sometimes sneered at. It's enough for me now to recognise – as long as there is a growth process going on, unfolding the potential of the inherent wisdom of deepest mind – that, like the unravelling of a serpent (good old *Shakti*, rising!), if the psyche is knotted, its unfolding has inevitably met blocks; and these blocks will clear themselves, gradually.

As long as the growth process is underway, it puts pressure on the blocks it encounters, gently challenging them to give way, so that its journey may continue. I will begin to understand that if I have a problem, it is not a problem with my father, but how I responded to him and how it has, until this time, blocked me from incorporating aspects of the masculine in my own expanding psychology. Fullness of being *insists* on growth.

Eventually you may reach the original knot. Psyche knows the nature of these knots. She is the repository of your stored experience; She has travelled with you all the way and, Goddess be praised, doesn't She have patience!

Out Uluru way ...

Back to 1986. *I hope you won't mind this flashback. It has acute relevance that resonates for years. The growth pathways link up experiences encountered in different zones.*

I take advantage of a hiatus between jobs to learn the techniques of *Reiki* healing from a visiting American, Beth Gray, a woman of indeterminate age, with white hair just like my own Yankee grammaw from Ohio. Beth is visiting Australia, teaching the Japanese *Usui* method for channelling healing energy.

The resemblance to my grandmother is particularly resonant for me, for it was she who once told me I would use my hands to heal. Grammaw used to read tea leaves and cards. She noticed my careful attentions with tiny budgie chicks who had been dislodged from their nest boxes by mother hens squabbling over preferred sites in the aviary.

I became surrogate mother to the rejected chicks. I would rescue them from the aviary floor, bring them into the house and, from a dropper, feed them seed that I had ground up in my own mouth, (mimicking the food regurgitated by the hens from their own crops). And it usually worked. They thrived on the attention, becoming absurdly tame, so at home indoors that they almost became a nuisance, especially for my house-proud mother who objected to their tiny droppings.

Beth Gray mentioned that during her Aussie travels she had visited Central Australia – something that I, and many of my coast-hugging compatriots have never done – and she recommended that if we were ever to go out to the red Centre, we ought not just visit Uluru (which used to be called 'Ayer's Rock', the name given by white explorer William Gosse in 1873 after Henry Ayers, the Chief Secretary of South Australia); we needed to make sure to also check out the low range of hills known as *Kata Tjuta*, which an early white explorer named Ernest Giles had named 'The Olgas' in 1872, after some European queen (Olga of Wurttemberg).

'That's the real *power place*,' she averred. And that memory lodged itself somewhere in my busy brain. Kata Tjuta.

A couple of years later in 1988 (I'm 43), I'm working as a segment producer on a late-night TV talk show, *Late Night Oz*, that is produced in Sydney and goes live-to-air nationally, Monday through Thursday nights, with Don Lane as host. We spend the Fridays locking in guests for the first days of the following week.

Out of the blue, I get an unexpected call from a firm of attorneys who are defending a case of alleged defamation brought against a Northern Territory newspaper by a chap who sometimes volunteered contestants for the talent quest segment of a show, *Young Talent Time*, a show that I had worked on previously, out of Melbourne. As the erstwhile producer of that show, they have singled me to give testimony as a witness for the defence.

I take time off work and fly up to Darwin, via Alice Springs, and I give my evidence under questioning on a Friday morning. Knowing I won't be expected back at work until Monday, I have the rest of Friday and the entire weekend free, so I book a side trip out from Alice Springs to the small airstrip at Yulara that services the trickle of tourists flying out to Uluru.

I book into the only motel and take the tour bus out to watch the sunset. The terrain is utterly unlike my usual city environs. All around, the desert floor is an impossible ochre red (not like my idea of 'desert' at all). For many of the coast-dwelling Anglo population, the deep interior of the continent has figured as an almost threatening presence, an environment only understood and survivable by indigenous folk. My own curiosity has lain dormant for decades but there is an opportunity and a mysterious synchronicity at work here, now, that feels like an imperative, as if I am to give way and cannot permit any further delay.

Busloads of tourists are gathered for the sunset viewing. The crowd consists largely of people from overseas countries, rather than your average Australians.

We are thousands of miles from everyday urban settings. The natural environment commands our attention.

Mesmerised, we watch in awed silence as the daylight withdraws and the huge rock displays its changing colours in the setting sun. Within that awe, I find myself subtly trembling.

I remember the *Reiki* teacher's admonition: Don't just stay with 'the Rock'. I'm determined to visit that other feature of the *Kata Tjuta-Uluru* National Park national park, the contrasting geological formation of low hills around 40 kms across the flat plain to the west. Next day, I check in to join a bus tour which takes us across the red plain, to a gorge known as the Valley of the Winds where we can walk in a short way. We are told that the indigenous people do not live here, but only come here for hunting and ceremony. Respect is the rule.

I've seen postcards of the area, and I want to enter more deeply into this mysterious terrain, but the tour bus schedule leaves us here for only a pitifully short time. We have to leave too soon to satisfy what has become a yearning for me.

The next morning, I board a flight for a helicopter flyover. In the early light I marvel at the soft grey appearance of the hills, completely mysterious and private in contrast to the striking boldness of Uluru. Extreme *yin* to its prominent *yang* presence. But I soon feel uneasy with my aerial intrusion, as if it is a violation, a form of tactless disrespect.

Back at the motel, I book to go out again on the morning bus tour, but I ask to be left out there all day this time and be picked up by the afternoon tour group, so I can linger and explore the whole day.

Supplied with a packed lunch and a large bottle of water from the motel, I am released from the morning bus, as agreed, to continue my explorations alone. I have all day to enter into the mystery. Trust has become unquestioned, a palpable imperative.

I soon find my way through to a walking track that leads across a flat valley floor. The interior opens up a much larger expanse of terrain than was obvious from outside and, as I pad along, I can only marvel at the intense silence that manifests in this pure natural environment, so utterly devoid of human constructions.

Soon, I find myself witnessing the reputed power at first hand.

My ears begin to buzz. At first, I accept this as the sound of cicadas that is common in the Australian bush. But the buzzing continues to grow in intensity, becoming ever louder and louder, forming an intense wall of sound that could surely only be made by millions upon millions of buzzing insects, if that were really the source?

The phenomenon increases to the point that I am slowed, then literally stopped in my tracks, by an overpowering sense of presence. I must allow my 'inner' ear to open, to accept the sound more fully into my being. It feels easy to slip into that gear as I have practised doing in countless seated meditations over the years to focus by listening within. It's an opening to a force larger than my puny self and it is the core of my being.

In this release I am impaled by an irresistible shaft of energy that enters through my head and earths itself through my feet. I'm skewered, surrendered to the profound power inherent in the primordial stillness of this stunning locale. It's like some kind of spontaneous initiation into a state of enhanced awareness, and it's happening alone, at a level of being I have until now always managed to overlook, except in small doses in the stillness of meditation. But this is deeper, an expanded virtual ground of being.

Perhaps the simple disciplines of the meditation practice have prepared my nervous system for this powerful infusion of energy, but to theorise or even conceptualise the experience is impossible; the part of mind that could operate through such framings has been thoroughly left behind.

On my walk in, I noticed some caves up the hill to my left and, when I can sufficiently collect my will, I crawl up towards one of these, where I am glad to simply sit. In letting go of the need to walk, meditation occurs easily of its own accord, the simplest state of being, but with eyes open, simply relaxing to observe the widest view of the scene spread out before me. My gaze relaxes completely, and I am quietly embraced, accepted ... It doesn't feel like I am intruding. I am profoundly at home here.

Among the dry scrub, I notice a stick of dry wood points up towards this cave, which I see now houses a small pile of firewood. And there is a sharp-edged rock here, too, from which pieces of flat stone have been chipped to make spearheads; for hunting I suppose.

I don't know how long I rest here. Peace prevails, inside out and all around. It is a peace that is pregnant with subtle power. I wander quietly for the remainder of the day. Far removed from the familiar environs of civilisation as I have come to know it, I feel deeply contented in this space, without any human intervention.

Even during the days of psychedelic experimentation, when I would hug trees, trying earnestly to connect with the natural world, I never felt so profoundly at ease because, I suppose, I wasn't secure in my own centre. All my life I have felt myself cast beyond the acceptance that comes so easily to people more aligned with the 'normal' parameters of conventional society. Here, a subtle and at the same time, powerful shift is occurring at the base of being.

Later, I come across a waterhole where a wallaby is waiting, alert.

There are postcards with shots of water sheeting off the sides of Uluru itself, forming instant waterfalls. During the evening sunset viewing at the Rock, I mention to one of the locals that I would really love to catch that sight.

'Oh sure,' he snorts, 'It hasn't rained here for seven years!'

I reckon my chances are slim. And I am to catch a flight to leave tomorrow afternoon. But next morning, the sound of rain wakes me, early. I look out to see that a dense cloud, suspended over the Rock, is already dumping its load, and water is cascading down parts of the monolith.

The power of listening

Where does one file these experiences, as one goes back into the demands of everyday living and working? Many years later (approx. 2010), I am hired to do a short job for the Teaching & Learning Centre at the local university in Lismore. As each School is required to do an evaluation of its courses from time to time, they bring in someone from outside to run focus groups: interviewing students past and present about their experiences in various units they have studied here; administer questionnaires and write up reports to feed into the evaluation. I am enlisted to do similar work with the Gnibi College of Indigenous Education at Southern Cross, where you can study for a degree that focuses on indigenous issues, including the complex impacts of intergenerational trauma.

This is an important area of concern, given the painful history of colonisation in Australia, where white settlement has so brutally displaced indigenous culture. The impact on families is severe and has continued across generations.

In addition to listening to students' experiences I do interviews with members of the teaching staff, and I take the opportunity to delve deeply into various subjects with the soon-to-retire head of the School, Professor Judy Atkinson. I am impressed not only by the mix of students' ages, ethnicities and previous educational backgrounds but their unusually high commitment to the materials and processes involved in the areas of study available at Gnibi.

I come across references to an indigenous practice of 'deep listening', known in some tribal languages as *dadirri*. At first, I took this to signify the respectful attention paid to whomever might be sharing their personal stories, in the sense that Buddhist Teacher Thích Nhat Hanh refers to:

> Deep listening is the kind of listening that can help relieve the suffering of the other person.
> I can call it compassionate listening. You listen with only one purpose: help him or her to empty their heart. And if you remember

that you are helping him or her to suffer less, then even if he says things full of wrong perceptions, full of bitterness, you are still capable to continue to listen with compassion. Because you know that listening like that, with compassion, you give him or her a chance to suffer less. If you want to help him or her to correct his perception, then you wait for another time. But for the time being you just listen and help him or her to suffer less. One hour like that can bring transformation and healing.

And I think of the listening I practised every day in our *satsang* meetings, where we learned to listen from our simple hearts as fellow devotees testified of their own heartfelt journeying. In both cases, the heart is open in empathic attention.

The term originated from the languages of the Daly River region in the Northern Territory and one definition gives its meaning as 'inner deep listening and quiet still awareness and waiting,' and another says it's a process of 'listening to learn.'

As my recognition of the term deepens, I begin to understand that it has an even more particular application to a deep inner spiritual practice. As I've explained before, I have been meditating under instruction from a young guru, who was born in the north of India but now teaches across the modern world.

Here I suspect that the *listening* also applies to being on country, a deep listening to become aware of presence without the incessant demands of ego in the way, patiently waiting for reality to show itself more deeply, feeling the simplest connection in kinship with the land and all its creatures. Is this what Thich Nath Hanh called 'inter-being'? Almost immediately I come across references to the practice in two novels written by indigenous people, notably in Melissa Lucashenko's *Mullumbimby*, and the intriguing book, *Earth*, by Bruce Pascoe, where *dadirri* is referenced.

Sometime later I am lucky to catch an industry screening of the movie *Charlie's Country*, which stars the powerful indigenous actor David Gulpilil, directed by the filmmaker Rolf de Heer who had excelled with previous films dealing with Aboriginal experience (*The Tracker* was one, *Ten Canoes*, another.) The tragic sense of displacement from 'country' haunts this later film and the long-term aftermath of white settlement as it is reflected in Charlie's world makes uncomfortable and deeply moving viewing. No wonder then that indigenous people often go into deep despair to be encased in a prison cell, cut off from their country.

There are several occasions when the dialogue stops and the action does, too. In these moments, director de Heer leaves the camera in close-up on Gulpilil's face; long sequences that allow the actor, in complete stillness, to take the viewer into his felt experience. His face is a window, drawing me into the depth of feeling that flows as a profound undercurrent to the silence.

Viewing becomes a virtual *listening* that, through respect, opens into the dimension of being-not-doing that is so readily sacrificed by everyday living and doing; a profound awareness of unity recalled in a stillness, in which there is no sense of separation. Here are the invisible roots of an ancient culture now almost totally bulldozed by white settlement, a coherent, integrated worldview all but obliterated by contemporary ignorance.

In these sequences it seems to me that Gulpilil is showing us *dadirri* in practice, embodying the profound humility required to find one's way back to a state of being where a deep sense of *belonging* to country, rather than indulging in the delusions of *ownership*, reveals something of its timeless wisdom.

This offers a different consciousness of relationship with place than the 'white' settler mentality trains us into. In a sense this is a passive, or more correctly, a receptive state of Being; one too easily overrun by a dominant, aggressive, materialist 'civilisation' which rudely pushes aside indigenous values. When indigenous people say 'I belong to country', the words point to a comprehensive set of values that are in direct contrast to a society based on *owning* land.

Is the tide beginning to turn now, where the environmental effects of such arrogance are writ large for all (or at least some) of us to see? An area close to the wilderness of Kakadu National Park was cleared to make way for the mining of uranium and now leaves the area dangerously irradiated with nuclear waste. Sites sacred to indigenous people are bulldozed ... Is it time to listen to what these humble people are trying to share with us?

I know that well-meaning people blather on about learning from indigenous culture, and waves of interest in traditional arts practices, etc., have risen and fallen as commodities, in the commercialisation typical of an acquisitive mindset. Even overwhelmed by a collective sense of guilt for our colonial history I wonder will it ever be more than a delicate dipping of one's toes in the water?

I wonder what we of the dominant culture would have to give up, to engage with indigenous beliefs and practices?

We urbanites may shudder at the prospect of initiation rituals rumoured to involve crude circumcision practices, or the impossible task of learning languages already disappearing beneath the waves of change ... and so on. Does this ever go beyond a kind of sentimental lip-service as we sip another Chardonnay and applaud these artefacts from the safety of our designer living rooms? I think it does, and there are more and more people eager to turn their attention this way.

So why is it important to me, this encounter with an indigenous practice?

I believe that *dadirri* calls to the receptive heart. Listen. While I may be treading in treacherous territories of cultural appropriation, I feel that for all the rhetoric about learning what indigenous teachings might offer white fellas, there could be a gentle opening up being enacted now. Let those with ears to hear ...

The busy mind misses so much, needing to be 'heard' against the silence.

I seek out references to *dadirri* on the Internet and come across the gentle teaching of indigenous woman elder Miriam Rose Ungunmeer Bauman, or Aunty Miriam Rose as she is sometimes known. She identifies as Christian and paints and writes. And I find her poetic evocation particularly resonant here:

To know me is to breathe with me
To breathe with me is to listen deeply
To listen deeply is to connect.

Her voice is not assertive. In its deep gentleness is an implicit invitation, an ancient culture reaching out to us to learn to listen, to hear and to share in its wisdom. How far has she come to speak to us? How far should we be prepared to travel into respect, even humility, to be receptive to its teaching?

When I open to deep listening, in the glistening silence of peace that I find in my meditation practice, I feel that the *Silence listens to me*, listening ... Two hands come together, folded respectfully in a gesture of greeting. Deep listening, surrendered without expectation, loosening the grip of that tight sphincter, me, and everything is, just as it should be.

I can listen, but what do I have to let go of, in order to hear? It is an internally centred process, leading me to the root of *being, rather than doing*, a deep listening stripped of ego, and a quiet, still awareness that recognises the wellspring that is the root of being, inside me. We call on it and listen as it calls to us. This is the gift that Australia is thirsting for, introduced to me by a young guru who came out of India, responding to my deep inner yearning, and I am embraced in a unity that is not merely constructed by custom and social conventions.

So, perhaps you will understand why this resonates so intimately with my growing insight into what Patti Miller calls 'the curious nature of being'.

The shift is occurring in my sense of being whole, at home in country, and in my own skin, being myself within the context of a much larger reality, not organised by a system of normative meaning that has judged me as some kind of marginalised 'type'. This shift has required me to relax my concept of who I am (often organised merely around a reaction to conventional constructions). Maybe this is beyond politics, or maybe it is the essence of politics, but in this environment all such notions fade, shift, and another, simpler reality asserts itself. The relationship between an 'I' and any ultimate context collapses into a new level of understanding.

Close encounters

Winter 2006. I'm sitting at my desk working on an article for publication. After the flood we moved the office out of the smallest bedroom and relocated it into the alcove off the kitchen. There are several unidentified cartons with random unsorted stuff tucked away around my feet.

I get up to go over to the kitchen for some water and a scratching sound catches my attention. I look down and there's a SNAKE! wriggling on the polished timber floor, trying to get away from me but gaining little traction.

How the hell did that appear, here?

No time for analysis, I'm freaking out! (And so is the snake.) I think it took a side swipe and might have actually bitten me out of shock. I'm wearing a pair of thick knitted socks from Nepal as slippers … do I feel a stinging in my right foot?

I'm still wondering how it got into the house as I head off towards the front entrance. There's a large rug near the front door that I might be able to throw over the reptile, which has headed over to an open space under the kitchen cabinetry. But when it sees me coming towards it, holding up a rug, instead of trying to escape, the brave critter comes straight towards me.

Faaark! I jump up onto a chair, still holding the rug, feeling slightly ridiculous, like the frightened housewife in a cartoon who jumps up on a chair to escape a mouse. This ain't no mouse, and it has aggressive intentions towards me!

The snake slithers off underneath a space where a pantry door doesn't quite meet the floor.

I seize the opportunity to push the rug up against that small opening, trapping the snake inside the pantry and grab the phone book to call a local wildlife rescue service for assistance.

A volunteer appears fairly soon and assesses my state of alarm. She is holding a strange lightweight caliper instrument in one hand, and a cardboard carton in the other. As she approaches the pantry door she instructs me to stand behind her and tells me that, if the snake comes out of the door, to 'stand still and DO NOT MOVE', no matter what.

Are you kidding me? Do not move?

She opens the door and I can see that the frightened snake has crapped itself. Using her caliper device the rescuer adroitly pins the snake against the back wall of the shallow cupboard, whereupon it immediately proceeds to curl itself up around the caliper which the woman is holding out in front of herself as she proceeds to manoeuvre the reptile into the carton.

I am relieved that no other confrontation arose for me to have to negotiate.

I ask her what species of snake we have captured, and she says she will have to call me later, when she works out which of two possible culprits, one being a 'rough scale' and another a 'keel back' that both like to be near water. It's not immediately obvious to her which it is, but she assures me that only one of the two is dangerously venomous, while the other is less so.

I thank her profusely and make a donation to the wildlife carers charity.

No phone call ever comes back to identify the species. But I am pretty sure that she clearly had come *to rescue the snake from me*, in my agitated state, rather than the other way around.

A month or so later I have to go to Sydney and I stay with Craig Bennett in his marvellous house in Church Point, on the water, north of Sydney. I got to know Craig when he was working as a show-biz correspondent from Hollywood while renting a unit in the same complex where I lived in my condo.

Craig introduces me to his pets: A pair of pythons. He has had a friendly history of snakes as domestic 'pets' since his childhood. He brings them lovingly out of their large glass enclosure and invites me to stroke them, which I do, if only gingerly. We go back to the lounge room to watch TV and later, during a break I pluck up the courage to go back to visit them on my own. What are they doing? Their bodies are intertwined, and they are slowly turning, in some serpentine embrace. They are languorously making love.

Craig's whole property is surrounded in bushland, and I feel a gentle shift into a feeling of safety.

Back in Byron, I *know* my reflex of fear has shifted when I *nearly* step on a deadly taipan (or is it a death adder?) lying curled up to the side of the path in the bush, and I calmly step around it. On another occasion a brown snake passes by my feet, right where I am standing, in the dunes behind the beach at Brunswick Heads. On neither of these occasions do I feel a need to panic and alarm them.

Sometimes I take the dirt road behind the dunes that runs for several kms all the way from Brunswick Heads to Tyagarah (and the nude beach!) One day I come upon an extremely long black snake stretched out across the track from one side to the other, seemingly inert but far too big to ignore. Is it asleep? I stop to watch, keeping a respectful distance. A curious bush turkey comes by and checks it out too and decides that the better part of valour might just be discretion.

Twice, on the dog beach down the hill from my place, I come across sea snakes lying on the foreshore, skin hanging loosely around their bodies. They use the sand to assist the seasonal moulting process. In the water, they move much more fluently; while here on the sand they are almost comatose, which leaves them vulnerable. Until someone's dog comes up to check them out and they raise their head to hiss a wary warning.

When I first moved to LA I lived at the foot of the Hollywood Hills. I used to take walks up into Runyon Canyon, where there's a ruin of a house (apparently once owned by Errol Flynn). The rest of a large estate is now public access, and there are various walking tracks where people go to exercise their dogs. On one occasion I was walking alone and, rather than taking the beaten track, I decided to return by climbing down a rocky slope as an alternative route. There, less than two yards ahead of me, moving slowly across the track was a rather large rattlesnake. I simply stopped and watched her take her own time. This was her home and, on this occasion, I was the visitor.

Even further back to Melbourne – it must have been early in 1972 – I was living in Carlton and took a day trip up into the Dandenongs with another actor from the Pram Factory, Bill Garner, who was planning to visit an artist friend and his wife who lived in Emerald. I was still in my hippie drug phase and dropped a tab of mescaline and enjoyed wandering freely in what was mostly farmland. At one point I was sprawled in the dirt, allowing my body to feel a kinship with the earth, but Bill wasn't feeling the same pull and drew me out of my absorption to go back to the house of his friends.

We gazed at an unfinished painting on the artist's easel; a simple landscape of the fields and a hillside. I felt I could see that the painter was trying to reveal an underlying structure under what was only superficially obvious and visible to the naked eye. I thought he was receptive to my comments but I might just have been deluding myself under the influence of the mescaline.

In the late afternoon our gracious hosts treated us to some fresh homemade bread, slathered in honey. He took us outside to the large decking at the rear of the house where he was feeding a possum, which took food tamely from his hand. I was rather taken aback by the size of the creature up close. I was still in a heightened state and felt cautious, almost frightened, so I left them to it and withdrew.

After nightfall and a cosy stew of homegrown vegetables with herbs, our host invited me back out to the decking. There was something he wanted to show me ...

The possum was there, its eyes glowing in the dark, but it had retreated further away on the handrailing. From across the gap it *zapped* me (no other word available) and it was an unpleasant jolt of energy. I recognised that it was returning to me, in kind, what it was like for itself, as a sentient being, to feel my fear and my rejection earlier. It was a nasty feeling, thank you not!

I accepted this lesson from the natural world; that fear is not necessarily an appropriate response.

I have a different kind of response with trees on the golf course next to where I live (using *reiki* hands to set up a circular exchange of energy); with dolphins swimming in the same wave; and with the whales playing around our boat. Relaxing into a continuity of being; it feels like a loving acceptance.

I remember a high school biology textbook titled *The Web of Life*. And I notice that the Vietnamese Buddhist teacher Thich Nhat Hanh speaks about a central principle of 'interbeing'. As part of a discussion panel on television, a journalist named Narelda Jaobs, who reads the News on Channel 10, explains to other panelists from Christian, Muslim, Jewish and atheistic systems how her understanding is informed by indigenous spirituality, and she describes that unity awareness with a fluid vocabulary of gesture. The times are changing – albeit slowly – to allow a new vision to emerge in our crassly materialist culture.

I find a documentary video on You Tube titled 'The Animal Communicator', about a striking South African woman, Anna Breytenbach, which is extraordinarily moving. I try out her techniques for a few weeks when I am traveling and invite the people with whom I'm staying to watch the doco with me. When I visit Judy Turnbull in Gosford she expresses concern about a big, gruff Rottweiler in her neighbour's yard.

Judy's back verandah offers an elevated view of the bush setting which her house backs onto and they have set up moveable branches to swing out some food trays for groups of various chattering birds. Down to the right in her neighbour's back yard the Rotty rushes the fence when it spots a bush turkey, but it's frustrated by the fencing.

Once, at an early age when I stayed with a marvellous aunt who played piano, she sent me next door to ask to borrow a cup of sugar from a next-door neighbour and I felt apprehensive because I knew there was a dog there. The back door to the kitchen was at the top of a set of stairs and when I arrived, I looked up; the dog was waiting for me at the top of the stairs. Maybe its size was exaggerated by the perspective – it looked large and I was small – and I ran away in fear. Of course, the dog chased me and caught me as I skidded full length on a gravel driveway at the front of the house. I fell and it pinned me. I screamed blue-bloody-murder until someone came out to rescue me and take me away to safety.

At home, my brother's small russet-coloured dog Lassie was a sweet-natured companion to all of the family, and no threat to me, or anyone. That is, until I was awoken one night when she growled and barked to chase away from the back verandah a guy who was trying to peer into my sister's bedroom window. In most domestic situations, as family pets, dogs were familiar and accepting of all comers who were familiar family friends, so I never felt that fearful or threatened to relive that fear.

But in my early adolescence, when I was walking home from visiting a friend's house in the dark, a suburban dog's barking at me set off an involuntary fear response. For the first time I felt a weird sensation of my scalp crawling, as though my hair was trying to stand on end. I had to learn to recognise that as a symptom of a natural underlying fear, and reason with myself that in many situations, especially if it isn't a large animal, I could probably win in a fight. Not that I wanted to test it out in a real situation, but it helped me to control the fear response.

So all these years later, as the Rotty is barking next door , I learn I can listen to him and recognise his anger and frustration with the situation where he is housed. When he feels me acknowledging his emotional experience, even from a distance, he relaxes and for a short while we blink at each other, in sympathy. He knows I have heard him.

Every time I watch the doco with the 'animal communicator' I feel pretty chuffed.

But I don't notice how I have begun to sentimentalise the connection, until I stay with Julie Caddy on her rural property, in the Bunyip forest region, north of Melbourne, complete with an impressive mud-brick dome house, three horses, and species of parrots I haven't seen anywhere else.

Julie works the horses, training one to compete successfully in dressage, and takes them out on long bush treks with a group of other riders. She is watching out for weight gain on one of the animals that she has retired and won't let him eat as much as he wants.

I am feeling plumped up with the milk of human kindness and ask Jools if I can feed a treat to this one that is being 'deprived'. With her consent, I offer a bunch of sweet grasses from the stack she has stored in one part of the shed. Of course, I try out my new-found 'animal communicator technique' to listen to him, but this experienced old horse pops my sentimental bubble with a cynical message: 'Come on, Princess; just hand it over …'

Overall, I feel that these various experiences are inviting me into a calm sensitivity to the creatures I live among. Although I am still disturbed by cockroaches.

Rapprochement

I abandoned him to the care of his mother. Decades ago. My son David. Naturally I have regrets. No excuses, but yes, certainly remorse. But his life has gone on its own trajectory and, as the years pass, I receive only snatches of information about him. An aunt tells me that he plays lacrosse at State level, so he must be fleet of foot and eye, and he has taken to disappearing off on surfing safaris, often in very remote locations.

When I settled down into a longish, almost stable period, working in TV in Los Angeles, I started writing what became an entirely one-way correspondence by snail mail. My letters would go off into the void, without any response coming back, so it's as though I am talking to the wind. With no feedback loop, I can't tell what he is making of my longish screeds, but this has the curious effect on me that it's even more important to just tell the truth about my queer nature and my short time with his mum.

The best I can do at this point is to try to always let him know my current address in case he wants to get in touch, including my e-mail address. When I get a US 'green card' I nurture a fantasy that when he finishes Uni he might want to come to do some schooling in California and he could stay with me.

Nothing comes of any of this. Until I finally get back to Oz and move to Byron Shire. Not as far away as Perth, finally. If he's a keen surfer, will this be an attractive locale? Out of the blue comes an e-mail telling me that he will be in the Shire for a wedding. He's a musician. Byron is the home of a famous music festival, and I hope that this too might figure into his future. But he goes back to Sydney (that's where he seems to be based these days) and I live in fantasyland for a while longer.

But at least I have his email reply.

When I am preparing a paper for a conference that will be staged in Adelaide I book my flight via Sydney, with a short stopover before connecting through to Adelaide, and let him know that I could meet up with him during those few hours, if that would be interesting for him.

I hang out in Sydney for most of the day and we end up going for a meal at Bondi Beach, where we rattle off a highly enthusiastic, rapid-fire conversation. I have a photo of that occasion, and we each have gleeful smiles spread right across our faces.

On a later visit he chooses to stay in my house in Ocean Shores and I get the great pleasure to introduce him to my men's group. Watching him interact calmly with the other guys, I am filled with a totally unfamiliar sense of pride. The father admiring his son. He plays at an open mic. night at the Bangalow pub and, as he is tuning up his guitar he says:

'My father bought this guitar for me …'

If I could hide, I would. I am embarrassed to have any attention drawn to me. I want to just sit here in anonymity admiring this fine young man play. I am the father who abandoned my son, but he is not judging me.

I remember how that happened, the purchase of the guitar. I was in Los Angeles, he in Perth. I've been writing those letters that get no response, but I persevere. As his twenty-first birthday approaches, I want to mark it as significant, and I scrape together a thousand bucks and send it to him. Later he tells me that he had been admiring a fine second-hand guitar in a specialist music shop and Lo and Behold! My cheque arrived, and it was for the perfect amount!

Come as you are

Rooted as I am now in my so-called 'home country' I find it much easier to meet up with my Teacher at events staged in Southeast Queensland. Devotees have been developing a site for a conference, now named Ivory's Rock Conference Centre, for a few years before I first attend one of these events, that lasts for five days. It's named Ivory's Rock after a notable rock formation with a significance rumoured to be of special status to Aboriginal people.

In the first few years, volunteers planted something like 10,000 trees to regenerate the site which had been used for farming. Some features lent themselves as perfect setting for an outdoor amphitheatre, say. A meeting hall, toilet blocks designed to the highest standards for water conservation, and a circle of shop fronts fronting a covered pavilion.

There are campgrounds with varying degrees of comfort that are continually being developed and updated for successive events. There's also a fine dining restaurant (named Daya's after one of my Teacher's daughters), that not only offers service possibilities for willing volunteers, but a rare taste of luxury dining, in addition to other facilities for those of us on a simpler budget to enjoy a variety of food offerings.

At one of these events, I've been burning out, doing too many shifts at Daya's, the fine dining restaurant. After a morning event in the amphitheatre with Prem, there are two sittings for lunch, and another round for evening meals after the late afternoon event in the cooler part of the day. Those of us working at this restaurant are bused back and forth to prepare for the luncheon service then back for the afternoon event, then back again to do the evening meal.

At the close of one evening event there's an announcement that there will be an opportunity next day for *darshan*, one of the rituals more common in India than elsewhere. Here it's simply called a 'greeting line'. For a devotee it's a precious chance to come face to face with the Teacher, and express one's gratitude, one by one, rather than being just a face in the crowd. This is something special for me and I always look forward eagerly to these rare opportunities – there are so few of them – and they always leave me in an altered state, one way or another.

One theme that has featured during Prem's evening talk could be summed up as an invitation to 'come as you are'. I suppose it's intended to get us to relax and front up without expectations.

The next day we volunteers who are working at the restaurant are bused down to the site and we wait close to the front of the line, so we can get back to finish preparation for the lunch shift. We are told by the efficient 'security' staff to leave aside our hats, bags, etc. There are around 4 to 5,000 people at this event, all devotees, so to be close to the front of the line should get us back to the restaurant in good time. Before us are people with special needs who need to be assisted to walk through the line.

Music starts to emerge from the tent and my heart begins to tune up to the vibe that these familiar sweet songs of longing inspire. Ahead of us the line starts to move. Then for no apparent reason, the line stops moving just after it has started. An officious Brit. working in security tells us to sit down, without any information about how long the delay will be ... leaving me stranded in the midday sun without my hat. I start to grumble to myself and pull my shirt up over my head for protection. The work at the restaurant is demanding and my patience is wearing thin. We work through to midnight and need to be back up there around 8.30 next morning to set up for the lunch service, which would be okay, except that sleeping in tents in the Aussie bush in September, one is awoken very early by the cascade of bird songs that begin before sunrise. This is a delight to our many overseas visitors but I do need some sleep. The toilet and shower blocks include areas for washing clothes, and dryers are in demand early through late ... And public phones are available for making calls back home and some of our visitors like to talk, talk, talk ... and I grumble on, to myself in private, of course. I wouldn't want to disturb the peace!

By the time we are called back into line, I am fuming. My patience has long gone and the line is already moving inexorably forward, but I am *not ready*! This is not the mood I need to be in to face my Teacher! but I can't drop out of the line, because I will miss the transport back up to the restaurant. And I don't want to face him in a state of anger. I need to calm down and compose myself ...

I fold my hands in front of me, adopting the pose of devotion. But I'm a mess. And there he is! No-one ahead of me is blocking my view and he is looking right at me, with a look of great amusement (and a loving smile). And I fall apart.

Come as you are, indeed!

As the line moves on, every step brings me closer and he is laughing. I am laughing too! In front of him, I don't know where my hands are now; my mood has blown up, into intense joy, and Mister grumblepot Me is dancing, skipping, completely free.

On the bus ride back up the hill I sit alone, quietly oblivious of others, savouring privately the exquisite, intense state of bliss.

'Coming out' as a 'spiritual' portal

In researching the exegesis for my PhD, I discover a significant paradox. The disillusionment that many queer folk go through: their profound displacement – experienced internally and externally as a series of shocks to the otherwise comforting sense of belonging – strips away some pretty fundamental illusions about self and society.

Disillusionment might then be seen as a stripping away of illusions. And I find that in Buddhism, rather than reinforcing the security of the ego construction of selfhood that Western psychology might be prone to 'fix', there's a conscious courting of the deconstruction of delusion.

Finding oneself in a hostile climate often contributes to a disillusionment that reaches deep into one's sense of self and undermines the sense of ontological security at the deepest level. Where do I fit? Am I a fundamentally awful mistake? However, rather than merely reinforcing a sense of victimhood, I suggest that this very disillusionment may work, paradoxically, as an early initiation into the kind of process that I have re-framed as an authentic pathway for spiritual inquiry and, ultimately, of transformation.

As a working definition, here I am using 'spirituality' as a term to denote a penetrating inquiry into the nature of being. And like the chicken breaking out of its shell ...

In Buddhist terms, this would be called 'dis-enchantment' – a kind of breaking the spell, a 'de-programming' from the tacit discourses that hold the world (of meaning, and personal identity) in the particular configurations in which we habitually construct them. The disappointment and suffering produced by the discrepancy between our idealised expectations and the way things actually are, may produce an awakening of sorts, with dis-enchantment as a quality of mind to be actively cultivated in the service of the Liberation process. Hence this extract from the Buddhist monastic code (the 'Vinaya'):

> concentration for the sake of knowledge and vision of things as they are, knowledge and vision of things as they are for the sake of disenchantment, disenchantment for the sake of dispassion,

dispassion for the sake of release, release for the sake of knowledge and vision of release, knowledge and vision of release for the sake of total unbinding without clinging. [Thanissaro Bhikkhu, Buddhist Monastic Code Dhamma-Vinaya. Pitaka: Parivara XII.2]

In the religious context, for example, men in this situation learn from personal experience to read the discrepancy between the official rhetoric – 'we love everyone' – and the homophobic cultural practices stemming from, and authorised by, leading institutional figures (Cardinals, Archbishops, Rabbis, Mullahs, *et al.*) in much the same way, I suspect, that women might recognise a similar dissonance between the misogynistic subtext in a discourse framed entirely within, and authorised by, patriarchal practice and the contrary claims that we are all equal in the eyes of 'God'.

To ignore the subtext and take the rhetoric at face value, I might add, can be an error fraught with real danger for a naïve and trusting queer child who might miss the hostility masked by the rhetoric. For gay men become acutely aware of a range of possible attitudes towards them: ranging from a sort of uneasy liberal tolerance, all the way through to death by stoning. The murder of Matthew Wayne Shepard in Wyoming in 1998 was a tragic reminder that homophobia has real-world consequences. (Shepard was left hanging on a fence to die by his attackers. In her radio commentary Laura Schlessinger seemed to imply that Shephard had brought his fate upon himself.)

Unaided by the wisdom of metaphysical teachings, such an experience can leave one in a fragile state … Or it can produce anger, alienation, rebellion and so on, for a short while, or chronically, long term. But here's something else that might be going on. At the time I begin to recognise this as a kind of initiation, a spiritual initiation, if you like. Making way for consciousness to manifest itself; a new way for imagining – nay, realising – new outcomes as the changes continue to flow.

To develop possibly experimental neural pathways, Psyche is encouraged to shake off the crust of old ways of thinking, of being, of becoming. The comforting illusion that the world is equally welcoming to all kinds of people has been badly shaken, but something else can take the place of that fond delusion.

That kind of experience can make one very angry, even lonely, in a hostile universe – hence the 'stranger in a strange land' syndrome. On the other hand this might instead become a breakthrough; or a break*down* in trust that can become an unplanned break*through*. It has taken me this long to look at it properly. Wrapped inside that very thing that has been used to shame you is the integration that returns the power that was taken from you. You have to own that very rejection. You can stand alone and feel what you are, existentially, coming together in a self-acceptance which can be very healing, from my experience.

For here again is the paradox: owning that very thing that has been used to shame you, may aid your return to wholeness. Divided against yourself no longer, all your power is returned to you, and a healing journey begins; not one relying on a greater degree of social acceptance, unless you are really fortunate, but one beginning within yourself. I choose to be who/what I am, and I release myself from the shaming that I have internalised. Many so-called gay men can testify about a palpable energy that is released this way.

Do those old-fashioned Church-based teachings *require* you to feel divided against yourself to maintain their power over you? Is it possible to become a 'disobedient subject' of the toxic traditions that construct you this way.

Hidden here is the 'gift' of being 'gay'. So, coming out; or marrying your 'same-sex' partner; in the public attestation of being, the feeling of displacement is eclipsed as you begin to come into your own wholeness. Hence, 'coming out' can reconfigure what you have construed yourself to be and the shift reconfigured and utilised as spiritual portals. Alice had to take the grow small pill to gain admittance to Wonderland in Lewis Carroll's vision.

Oddly, I find over time that the more I accept, nay embrace the gift of being uniquely me, other people tend to find me easier to accept (surprise, surprise!) Sometimes I find that so-called 'straight' men even enjoy my company; that what some of them have been reacting to, and yes, wanting instinctively to attack, is what they feel as weakness, rather than gayness *per se*. Their crude form of masculinity has had them in some cases virtually 'holding their breath', defending themselves against the feared, allegedly, feminine aspects of their own being. Mixing with a men's group, composed almost entirely of others who identify as 'straight', helps me accept my difference, giving me more confidence, where before fear might have ruled.

Crashing the printer

2012

I'm teaching a class at Southern Cross university; a semester-long unit in Cultural Studies titled Gender, Sexuality and Society. Some of the students are taking the unit externally and some choose to meet face-to-face, where I will be the master of ceremonies guiding the undergrads through the curriculum. What do I know about the intersections of gender, sexuality? About society?

Yes, I have lived through some major changes on the level of social mores and in my own time. I'm nearly seventy years old. On this formal level, have I ever theorised that experience? Is raw experience enough to work from? And how do I teach what I have learned? I don't want to impose my 'conclusions' on these young folk. Can we walk through these doorways together?

The materials provided to structure the course are a very good guide but, as I prepare for the face-to-face encounter with these unsuspecting students, my anxiety levels are rising.

My solution is to prepare, obsessively. Perhaps unconsciously I want to flood the poor students' minds with information so they will be too overwhelmed to notice my insecurity? What's going on here? The teacher is a student too? Yes.

It's 4.30 a.m. I am at home, in the middle of preparing handouts to distribute for the two three-hour sessions that I need to lead today. The money is good, and I need a new water heater, but at what cost to my hard-won peace of mind?

I'm tensing up in anticipation. This is not the first time I've experienced this challenge, and I should know by now that working at a furious pace is not conducive to the smooth operation of equipment, especially electrical equipment …

And my bloody printer jams!

I open it up to clear the paper path. And then press PRINT, again. No luck! The computer is mocking me, still telling me to clear the paper path. Frustration swells.

Within a half an hour I have deconstructed the entire machine in my frantic need to get the damned thing to print the material I have spent so much time preparing. To no avail. Whatever is blocking the path will simply not be cleared. As my frenzy increases, I discover that I have actually destroyed the machine.

No handouts? How can I trust myself to survive a three-hour seminar? Twice. Impossible!

I get out to the university early. I've loaded my handouts onto a thumb drive. It's an hour's drive away. I'm hoping to access the Departmental printer room. But access to the printers is only available from a computer in a locked office and I don't have a key. I'm part-time; a so-called 'sessional' lecturer. And time is trickling away.

How soon will those students arrive?

My panic has produced a palpable physical sensation. A block is tightening in my neck and shoulders. Time to surrender, my friend. Pray for grace.

'Just do your best and let grace take care of the rest,' my Teacher has advised in other circumstances. How many times? You'd think I would have learned to stay in the flow, after all those occasions. I understand the theory; trust induces the grace to flow, gets little anxious 'me' out of the way, leaving room for assistance from the ultimate helper. Well, I've certainly done my best!

I ought to make a checklist for when I find myself in similar situations: Intention? CHECK! Preparation? CHECK! etc. I have destroyed the effing printer and will have to buy a new one. Hmmm. This reminds me of all those days and months and years on the road, giving *satsang* EVERY NIGHT and most days, in many different cities, when each and every time I had to let go and allow the flow to carry me. I remember one occasion – and one only in all those years – where I was choked by self-doubt and was unable to speak.

So I have to ask myself: Why do I divide these situations into separate realities now? The teacher (little me), and the students, ready to listen. Is it not time to do away with partitions? If I prep for a class, or a conference presentation, and I try to stick only to my script, what am I shutting out? Who knows what the Teacher of teachers – aka the Holy Spirit – wants to achieve in this place? Couldn't this be a way to serve, *every* moment, *every* opportunity, *every* encounter? I recall how the flow of *satsang* would take unexpected directions and how often someone would come up afterwards and say: 'That story you told was just for me'. Trust. *You are not the source*, Victor. And you are learning what is required to become 'the servant of the sacred' ... again; here in a classroom. How much do I habitually throttle the operation of Her greater intention?

The contrast is acute.

The word *enthusiasm* is Greek in origin: something about being filled with 'the Holy Spirit.' That work in a different setting trained me to let go and 'flap in the breeze' when I was on the road for months at a time, talking to people in different cultures, helping them make the inner connection through meditation, in each and every situation realising that to do the work I had to let go and trust. Does that really need to be banished, now, into the secular caves of oblivion? Listening quietly, I hear her, I feel her joy awakening, thrill to her loving breath. A trick cyclist from a circus in Vienna warns me that this is all wrong, that it's a regression to an infantile, irrational state. But he's the one who admitted he has never understood music, so what does he know? It seems to me that his fear-filled mind turned him deaf to her entreaties; he prefers to study pathology.

Dream jottings calling me inside to rest with fishes' watery languidity, playing against the tide: the stream of unconsciousness flirting to be heard/felt/known/whispered/voiced/sung!

As the students jumble into the room we face off, human to human, and for all my anticipatory fear, I let go ... and it flows, quite naturally. Human beings working together. And 'education' is a deeply joyous exchange!

Out of my way

So, I've been living in the Shire for around 5 years… My sister Val wins a voucher for a free consultation with a well-known naturopath and gifts it to me. Barry Donnelly has a practice up on the Gold Coast and one closer operating from his home, in Bilinudgel. He does his thing with some machine he uses for diagnosis. My symptoms aren't serious, I just feel tired all the time and I reckon there might be some malfunction of my thyroid gland.

He tapes electrodes to my scalp and, with my hands holding terminals and my bare feet placed flat on some metal pads, he hooks me up to a computer program and runs a current of some kind through the circuit.

'It's your adrenal glands,' he declares and shows me a read-out from the computer that is running some expensive diagnostic program. Some other details about heart and brain show up too. He explains that if the adrenals aren't functioning properly, they can throw out the other glands that form part of the endocrine system.

'This is why you feel tired all the time.'

I remember a phrase I heard when doing *Reiki* training years before, about 'adrenal insufficiency syndrome' but that's a serious condition, isn't it?

'My adrenals can't be buggered,' I say, 'I live in the Shire of Byron Bay, for God's sake!' It's a famous place for visitors to come and partake of one or another of the array of healing modalities on offer. It seems that every second person is a practitioner of some kind …

'Well, tell me, are you busy?'

I consider that possibility. Let me see, in the past five years I've driven north to Brisbane a lot to go to meetings with my thesis advisors; I've completed a PhD dissertation and published the first of three books. My house was flooded and I have spent a year in charge of the renovations, while keeping up the research and the writing, and so on. The penny drops – I have been rather busy, even in this erstwhile hippie haven, and it has been a tad stressful …

'There's a herb I'd like to recommend,' proposes Dr. Donnelly. 'You would take this mostly in the evenings, but not in the morning because it might slow you down a bit.' He writes down the name and recommends that I should take it in liquid form. *Rehmannia glutinosa*. He has some, right here on the premises. It's a big bottle and it is expensive in my reckoning, but the consultation hasn't cost me anything, thanks to Valerie's golfing prowess, so I hand over the money and agree to follow his advice.

Within just two or three days there's a palpable shift in my physical being.

I never expected that a single herb would produce such a notable effect, with my body going into a noticeable change of gear. Everything becomes much clearer. I can see ahead to the next few things I have to do, and I'm quite content to let them fall into place in an orderly, unrushed fashion. I get just as much done, but there's no pressure. How can this be?

I continue to take the herb and when the bottle runs dry, I get another. The calming effect continues.

Looking back at this now I see that I am gaining some insight into the way I habitually go at things. Despite the intellectual work and its challenges, I'm also impulsive and emotional. There's probably a personality category that fits me well, but I won't be satisfied with applying some rote theory; it's as though I am learning this experientially, and in my body, as lived experience, if that makes sense. My body is the sensor, the 'canary in the coalmine', and if I can just attend with conscious awareness to its innate intelligence ...

This all ties into the meditation practice that my beloved Teacher has been patiently guiding me into over decades. The deeply contented state that clears the mind (note, it doesn't just send me to sleep, or 'turn me into a vegetable', as suspicious commentators would have it!) is an everyday reminder of the value of a calm state of clarity, where I don't get ahead of my breathing. Now if my planning gets all bunched up, especially during really busy times, which is how it feels, I treasure the quieting that takes place even more. I can see more clearly, even think things through one step at a time, which is a valuable shift in habit for such an impulsive type as me!

Ultimately, I even come up with a little slogan to remind myself. It goes something like this: 'When human doing takes a break, human being is waiting there just to embrace me.' From that state of being, my mind and actions are less cluttered.

On the Internet this reminder from the timeless poet Rumi:

> When I run after what I think I want, my days are a furnace of stress and anxiety; if I sit in my own place of patience, what I need flows to me, and without pain. From this I understand that what I want also wants me, is looking for me and attracting me. There is a great secret here for anyone who can grasp it.

Transitions

Finally, after a year of trying to sell the house, we have managed to get a buyer. As much as we have done to improve the property – including the second renovation, post-deluge – we haven't made a lot of profit, for we feel obliged to inform each potential buyer that without some engineering work by the Council to avoid future flooding we can't really be sure whether the next major flood event would come in fifty years, or much sooner.

A buyer is satisfied, finally; a date arranged for settlement, and I began the search for another dwelling, preferably on higher land, or at least away from the water. With a deadline now put in place by the settlement date on the house, and a budget determined by how much cash I can now call upon, the hermit crab must move his dwelling again.

At this point in my life, without a job or income, I am both unable and unwilling to commit to a mortgage. I can't afford city prices and I like living here on the coast. But here, the price of actual stand-alone houses is already beyond reach.

My sister is living with her partner, Judy – another avid golfer – in a solid, brick-built complex of apartments, or villas, adjoining the 'Country Club'. Do I want to shrink my living space? Do I really have any choice?

Judy points out the advantages. She doesn't need to tell me about the views; they overlook the ocean. 'You could invest in one of these units?' she proposes gently. 'There's a strong body corporate, with a good emergency fund …'

The units don't often come onto the market but when they do, given these advantages, they usually sell quickly. The first one that becomes available is already beyond my budget. I would rather live in a house than a unit in a complex anyway, so I spend two weeks looking at properties, far to the north – preferably not in Queensland, where the politics are dicey (although New South Wales hardly passes muster) – and as far south as Ballina, as well as further inland towards Federal. But houses prove way too expensive and many of the flats are simply depressing, with their low ceilings and pokey internal spaces.

Living in this area, I have come to enjoy the company of my remaining sibling, my conscientious, heart-centred, sister Valerie – after years, continents, even oceans apart. So, when an affordable, smaller unit finally does become available, in the middle row of their complex, I cave in to their gentle suggestion and agree to take a look. It's not large, with only two bedrooms and a tiny galley kitchen, and the entrance is through the garage; so it isn't perfect. But it has vaulted ceilings and a very wide balcony, with exceptional ocean views to the north and east. For one person, it's probably perfect. *Surrender*, Victor! It's staring you in the bloody face.

I haggle to get the price within reach and to time the settlement to occur on the same weekend as the house I'm leaving. I should have enough left over to buy a new computer, update my eyeglasses and buy a new fridge to fit into the narrow kitchen. There's no stove, which they have neglected to mention, so I hunt around for an affordable combined microwave/convection oven. Given the tiny kitchen, I won't be throwing any dinner parties.

I miss the large interior expanses of the house we renovated on Orana Road – I thought I would end my days there – but the decking and the views here more than make up for that change of plan. And I'm top of the hill, instead of in the flood plain, so why have I been dragging my feet?

After a garage sale to clear what will not fit into the new abode, I use Val's sturdy 'ute' to shift essentials into the new place. The timing is acute – I have to get everything out of the house we're selling in time for settlement on the modest villa, so everything has to be completed now! The move is a huge effort physically and, notwithstanding my innate tendency to go like a bull at a gate at physical tasks, I try to pace myself. But I reverse the tow bar of Val's vehicle through the timber wall of the garage, leaving a tell-tale, ball-shaped hole – a fact that I manage to hide from her for several months.

I don't know when I will ever settle into a truly harmonious rhythm and allow things to unfold in patience. My back tightens up considerably during the move, of course, (all that lifting and carrying), and it takes some careful, conscious unwinding to un-clench the muscle strain of my lower back. But over the first few weeks a series of sweet, deeply peaceful meditations make settling in a virtual dream. I slowly surrender to the presence of the ocean's beneficent power and find myself in a renewed state of wonder. The peace here is palpable!

Again, I have to recognize through the wisdom of the body how action/effort/will is so often, in my case, inextricably tied into this clenching tendency that affects my lower back. In one morning meditation, I finally accept the peace on the inner and outer planes and I am undone, loose as a wet noodle. I pray that I could go through the day without at any time needing to leave this state of un-doing. Wu wei, in Taoist terms, I suppose. When not sure of the theory, doing is teaching in action? *Even while doing, one finds a way to not be doing.* Human being or human doing? Human being, in action, rather than crude either/or.

It's September 2007, the year of my graduation ceremony for my PhD.

The second bedroom becomes my study – I'm working seriously on my first book …

Magpie's song

My home base now is this north-facing apartment in a complex on the side of a hill up near the golf course, with a view overlooking the houses on the street below, down to a river – Marshall's Creek – and across a nature reserve, all the way down to the ocean: New Brighton, my local beach, where I was welcomed by two dolphins on my very first visit.

The sun rising over the ocean wakes me early and travels through the day to set spectacularly behind the mountains to the west. We abut a large 18-hole competition golf course (where my sister keeps winning championships) and in the afternoons, the light through the clouds and the tall eucalypts is like a farewell blessing.

Sometimes I can spot whales, from the vantage point of my broad balcony. One season they head north to warmer waters to birth their calves; in spring, they head way back down south to scoop nourishment from the teeming krill of the southern oceans. Neighbours and even passing strangers share their glee and pass on early news of cetacean sightings off the beaches.

Valerie takes me and her partner Jude out on the water for a close-up view and we are shaken to the core of joy as some of them actually break their journey and double back to follow our boat, diving underneath to appear the other side, as we rush back and forth across the deck. A young calf shows off its prowess, leaping full-length out of the water alongside the length of the boat and we whoop our applause.

In an earlier part of the century Byron Bay used to have a whaling station; but something has shifted over the years. Despite the cynical appraisal by some sophisticated city folk, Byron is not overrun by nutters, and I would bet that if they came into a close up with one of these gentle giants, they too would feel the thrill. My connectedness with the natural world grows ever stronger.

The golf course teems with bird life (and snakes). In the early mornings the tweets, trills, screeches and snuffles of so many species keep the natural world pressed up against my attention. And day and night, the sound of the ocean is sighing in the near distance. I am not troubled by traffic noise, for my narrow street – barely an alley width –

is one-way; and not a road through to anywhere, it's a loop. Often the stillness of the place becomes so prominent that I am drawn spontaneously into meditation and I find myself literally basking in the quiet.

One morning I notice a young magpie perched atop a neighbour's rooftop aerial, stark against the early summer sky. He's busy chortling and trilling, trying out phrases, new songs, and he seems lost in the discovery of what he can produce. He's like a young jazz musician, riffing on the possibilities of joy. Yes, joy. It's pure pleasure for him to improvise these songs, and he carries on, delirious, for more than an hour, undisturbed in his private rehearsal.

In a library book *The Australian Magpie*, I discover that for a young bird to discover its voice like this, he has to separate himself from the rest of his crew for his innate talent to develop. They use chambers in their young bodies (these are not like our larynxes but small, bellows-like sacs) to produce the sounds their songs need to articulate. If these resonators are not exercised when they are young, they simply do not develop.

I write a short poem about this encounter, trying to fit it into the Japanese tanka form and I take several versions to a workshop run by a local poetry group, to try it out. It goes something like this:

There, on the wire of my neighbour's rooftop aerial,
stark against an early summer sky,
the young magpie riffs, delirious
with the possibilities of joy.

But I am earnestly advised by the most experienced poets among the gathering:

'It wasn't the magpie that was feeling joy ...'

I blink back at them.

'*You* are the one experiencing joy; it's not the magpie. The magpie is just a magpie.'

I am surprised. I knew the youngster was enjoying himself as he tried out his improvisations, but the proper poets are unanimous in judgement. Have Calliope, Erato and Euterpe all abandoned the field in this modern colony of Rational Materialism?

Back at the apartment complex, the chairman of the Body Corporate comes to my door to advise me that there is a move on to 'clean the place up' and that I am being 'targeted' (that's the language he chooses.) My sister's partner, Judy, has set up a system of wires as an espalier to support a flowering vine. The offending vine grows along the top of the brick wall that encloses the small courtyard at the front of my place, and it spills some of its foliage and its seasonal flowers in a way that obscures the 'clean' lines of the bricks.

'But who has complained?' I ask. The Chairman is taken aback by the assertive nature of my request for information, and his tone shifts defensively. 'Targeted' is the language of warfare, and I bristle. I've been going about my days unaware that there is cause for tension.

What is the need for such precise conformity in this zone that I inhabit? Am I surrounded? I suspect that he is the only one complaining.

He declares, too, that the tiny plot of garden alongside my driveway, wherein the offending vine is rooted, is not technically 'mine'; it 'belongs' to the Body Corp., and their gardening committee wants to control what may or may not be planted there. They chop away the top layer of a desert plant too, that is well accustomed to the soil conditions and has grown past the line of bricks.

Really! Has all the lyricism of life itself been extirpated? Do bricks have more rights, more inherent value, than greenery and blossoms? Have I gone mad? In my internal monologue, I dub him and his cronies the 'brickheads'.

Nearby, at the top of the golf course, some thirty metres away, there is a magnificent stand of eucalypts, where magpies gather and sing. The gardening faction hack off high branches to protect inmates of their 'brickfields' from risky branches in the trees, and they clear away more shrubs in the name of tidiness.

Sterile order reigns.

I read a study put out by the CSIRO that has been written by a woman who is an expert in the field, Gisela Kaplan. Prof. Kaplan notes that as one of our nation's most popular and iconic birds, it is loved for its impressive vocal abilities, propensity to play, excellent parenting and willingness to form enduring friendships with people. A magpie warbles on my front balcony and when I work out that he is asking for a treat, he later brings members of his family along to enjoy what's on offer.

I quit the poetry group but I continue to try out different variations.

Transitions of another kind

While re-connecting with my sister, I have come to know and admire the dynamic woman whom she has taken as a partner. Married three times previously, Jude tells me that she is in love, *for the first time*. At the golf club, tongues were wagging. While Val has earned their grudging respect with her golfing prowess, Jude already has that respect as one who persevered against the odds.

She has survived two previous bouts with cancer and powered on as an independent businesswoman, taking over the suburb's first news agency. In turn, she adds a post-office branch, and a lottery franchise, in the process earning the wider community's gratitude for her hard work and business acumen. When a breast cancer scare requires surgery, people volunteered to keep up the early morning paper delivery route and Jude has weathered the storm courageously.

She asks me about meditation, and I have to put her off. Even though I still practise every day myself, I am no longer 'licensed' as an instructor and I try to point people towards my Teacher, which is a little trickier. Some of them do make the shift from me to make their own connections with him but that can take time, especially when they are as busy as Jude.

I tend to ask people: Are you a human *doing*, or a human *being*? Not one or the other, in mutual exclusion, but in Jude's case – she's a fighter! – she's committed to one mode, and I can understand why. She de-stresses by getting drunk, bless her, but that's not perfect preparation for meditation.

Late 2008, moving into 2009

A year after her second mastectomy, doctors discover a troublesome new cancer, this time in the bowel, and Jude is scheduled for surgery, early in the new year. She detests hospitals and cuts her stays there as short as medically feasible and checks herself out on a Friday, armed with two chemo prescriptions to carry her through, post-op.

One of the meds seems to have a speed-inducing side effect. Never one to sleep much, Jude is immediately out practising her golf swing and playing tennis on the road with the dog. This is perilous activity for someone recovering from abdominal surgery, but you can't keep a good woman down!

On Monday morning, around 7.05 am, I get a call from Val. 'Come quick', she urges, 'It's Jude.' Instant emergency! Their place is very close by and I'm there before 7.10. Jude is parked on the loo. But her lips are turning blue, and Val is trying to lend her breath, and is attempting to palpitate her chest.

I find myself calling her not to leave. A long time coming to this acute crisis, but now it's so sudden.

Val has already called the ambos and they arrive at 7.15.

'She's gone,' they pronounce, and we look on in disbelief. Within an hour her local doctor comes by and asks us to describe what has happened. From the blue lips and the apparently sudden departure, the doctor reckons that she has bled away internally.

Val and I are left stunned.

Was it too much activity so close to surgery? Had she ruptured the stitches internally? The doctor writes out a death certificate.

Jude has left instructions that her body be made available to medical science, but we have to wait to connect with the correct Department north of the border, in a different time zone. By the time we hear back from them, they have decided that given her history of chemotherapy, they cannot accept the body.

For the next few hours we continue our vigil without interruptions. Val is weeping quietly, gently holding her lover's body. I have been drawn into meditation. In that state I can see that Jude's energy is circling, disturbed, in her lower body, and I am 'seeing' that as colours swirling, in her aura.

Hell! What am I saying? I have not been trained for this.

Even though she has been declared officially dead, I intuitively get that she has not 'left' yet, and further, that she is in a state of alarm, plainly disturbed that she cannot get her body operating …

I'm drawn to lay my hands upon her as I had learned through *Reiki* and somehow allow peace to be drawn into the situation.

I haven't forgotten that she asked to learn how to meditate and I wish that had come about. But she has always been so busy. However, during my own practice over recent weeks I have been noticing a shift, whereby the techniques that I have used for years, day in and day out, are activated spontaneously. As if meditation is 'doing' itself.

My senses have tended to withdraw and inverted my attention, with no effort on my part. The top of my head, particularly, has been stimulated, subtly but quite distinctly, and there's a kind of channel drawing my attention in and up, behind the eyes, as though my entire being is being guided up and out of my body, even while being anchored, paradoxically, in the physical, *through my hands now*. Is this what is meant by 'channelling'?

I lay my hands in some of the positions I learned through *Reiki*, years before, and the feeling in this apartment settles, energetically, even as the ocean sighs onto the sands of the beach below. At one level, I don't know what I'm doing; but I'm feeling a profoundly calm energy – a kind of transcendental love that is older, deeper, wiser and familiar – that allows a deep atmosphere of peace to envelop us all.

This is how a roomful of people would settle as we gathered into meditation together when I was playing the role of instructor all those years ago.

Jude's faithful dog, Saffron, is drawn into what is occurring. She comes over to systematically lick Jude's body. First, she goes to the left hand, then to her left foot, then moves across to finish her lapping at Jude's right hand before returning to rest on the sofa.

I am not in control of what's happening, but my meditation takes charge of me, bringing me into alignment, and the *Reiki* practice I am guided to do transfers the deeply calming energy to Jude.

I can see and feel that her spirit is now settling. Her aura appears to have resolved and, after some time has passed, I notice that all the colour in her body has collected at the top of her head (which has been shaved previously during the chemo) like a caul, and I see that now as a shade of purple.

Thank Goddess that, even with all my wondering, the *Reiki* and the meditation combined keep me out of the way. I am an observer to a deep and natural transition, even while I am somehow able to assist. Can one really be a 'midwife' to the dying?

It reminds me of those years on the road, teaching the meditation practices on behalf of my Teacher, Prem. Once all the preparation had been completed, and all the words run down, it's as though I was overshadowed and the practices virtually imparted themselves, with only minimal instruction from me. It was a strange state of mind, but I experienced it again and again and again, over weeks and months, even years, in so many towns and cities. Getting me out of the way. Making me simple. Allowing a natural process to take place.

To be there, and yet not be there, with the deep, subtle energy of a special quality of peace running the whole show.

I begin to wonder if there's something that I need to do, to somehow bring the process to its conclusion. I've read in a Buddhist book about the 'spirit', or soul; whatever, departing ideally through the top of the head. I also recall hearing that it was very bad form to touch a Buddhist's head, and I wonder if this applies here.

While I am still wondering, Jude's dog comes over to where we are sitting and begins to vigorously lick the top of Jude's head.

How does she know what to do?

In the end, peace prevails. We have, all of us, been brought together in service to a primal event and it has drawn us into a state of wonder and simple, unquestioning trust.

Once again, I have been painted into a corner, forced beyond what I know on one level, yet required to be present, to operate in a subtle extra dimension, despite my ignorance; and something profoundly natural has taken place.

Two weeks later, devastating bushfires destroy some towns in the Victorian bush, and I read how some victims of the blazes died in frightful circumstances. I start to understand what it might mean to have a 'fortunate death' and offer a quiet prayer that their souls might find peace.

Much later, I come across a statement from the Tibetan teacher Sogyal Rinpoche (it's the reading for March 20, in his book *Glimpse After Glimpse: Daily reflections on living and dying*), to the effect that, at the moment of death our state of mind is all important and the last emotion that we have before we die 'has an extremely powerful determining effect on our immediate future'.

Acceptance

September 2006

The time has come and the thesis has to be brought into a form to present to examiners. The scholarship money is about to run out and my newly-arrived research advisor is still managing left-overs from his last position. He does a read-through of the memoir in draft form and hasn't the time to read my 'exegesis', so he will be little help during this critical final phase.

'Let's take a break and get ready to submit in a few months' time,' he suggests.

However, one of the brilliant women in the School takes an interest and recognises what's needed. Dr Ruth Blair has been teaching courses in American literature and is a renowned authority on Herman Melville, among other things, and she has brought others' postgrad. theses to successful completion. She's just going into retirement but, Goddess be praised, finds my project interesting enough to pick up the slack and help me slap my project into final shape.

I've complained to Amanda Lohrey (since retreated to Tasmania) that the exegesis – the theoretical discussion to accompany the creative work – has taken over and I still haven't finalised *The Boy in the Yellow Dress*. In her typically perspicacious way Amanda wisely suggests that I should 'go where the oxygen is', so I have allowed the exegetical study to run its course.

An excellent critical reader, Ruth takes a beady-eyed look at what I've written for the exegesis. 'Stop working', she advises, 'this is good, but it's repetitive, here, and here …'

Ruth to the rescue! Just another one of the series of meetings with remarkable women that I can never take for granted. We decide that I will present a 'potted' version of the memoir and proceed to prune back the over-long exegesis, presenting the total package as a kind of diptych; the themes of the memoir are argued out in depth in the formal study, which focuses on Isherwood as my main case study. QED.

Ruth is an adept reader and slashes back part of the guff to make the whole thing hang together better. I relax a little under her guidance, especially when I realise that a supervisor's 'reputation' is on the line if they present a work for external examination with experts from other universities. I do the work – I've already done the work, in fact – and when satisfied, Ruth gives it the supervisor's seal of approval.

In December of 2006 when I finally do submit the project for examination I walk around as if in a daze. A palpable light-headedness continues for several days. I simply haven't recognised how the intense mental concentration has dominated my time and my energy. I feel that I don't care very much what the external examiners' verdict will be (it will take around three months, I am told). I've brought the project to a conclusion. I've achieved my goal.

In March the following year the examiner's reports come back and they are positive. The University needs me to lodge bound copies for the main research library, complete with a digital version on a CD, plus additional hard copies for my School, and for my 'supervisors'. The central thesis office stamps them, declaring the work 'Accepted for the degree of Doctor of Philosophy'. Crikey!

My overall title is 'The Journey of the Queer 'I': Spirituality and Subjectivity in Some Life Narratives by Gay Men' and I wonder how it will find its place among other impressive work done in the Sciences, and other more respectable disciplines.

I go around to deliver the copies to various offices, and the task is finally complete. I go down to the ferry stop on the river and cross over to West End, where I walk slowly up to the house where I am staying. I feel utterly spent, exhausted on more than just the physical level. Lying on my bed for several hours, I find myself weeping.

I don't really understand what's happening, but in that altered and highly emotional state, I hear the voice of a small boy, asking 'Are you proud of me now?'

Choosing love

Melbourne, 2014

I'm in Melbourne, in a radio studio being interviewed (94.9 JOY FM) during a book tour promoting my memoir *The Boy in the Yellow Dress*, which has finally been completed, edited, and published. The book on Isherwood, my exegesis, has beaten it to the post, in 2010 as *Mr Isherwood Changes Trains*, as has the collection I pulled together on the subject of marriage equality, *Speak Now: Australian Perspectives on Same-Sex Mariage*, in 2011.

One of the radio hosts suggests with all that traveling I must have had a lot of sex (all over the world) – it is a 'gay' radio station after all. When I demur (for much of the time while travelling, I was living as a modern-day monk, after all, teaching an ancient meditation practice) she confirms that I am currently 'unattached' and alerts listeners that I will be at the book launch at the bookshop in Fitzroy in a few days' time. She's trying to set me up! ... And I play along, tamely! After all, that's what defines us, isn't it, the great god Sex? How do I fit into that, supposedly playing the randy 'sexual deviant'?

Afterwards, I regret missing my chance to assert what I was really doing when I was touring around as a modern-day, plain-clothed monk. And the reality of the feeling that I carry today is that I am always, already, perfectly loved, at the deepest level of being. That love itself is the source of being; that breath itself is the sign of the Creator's love, the birth into being here, now. That the sign of God's love in me is the breath – sine qua non! – without which NOT! Before anything else, there is breath; the one essential for existence in this form, yet the most overlooked and taken for granted.

Is it heretical in queer culture to say that all partial identifications, including 'gay', are not the whole story? And should I have affirmed that one can be in a state of love at any time, anywhere? I recall an ironic questioning from Krishnamurti that while we might 'go to the well of love, are we carrying only a thimble?'

Rather than playing the game – that love is the thing that we only get to explore in the intimate frisson of skin-to-skin stimulation – why not get in touch with that reality? Because that is what is fundamental.

I admire those writers like Christopher Isherwood who found a way to pursue spiritual study with his guru, without repudiating his sexuality. I'm the guy who was often less than content to be 'looking for love in all the wrong places', when what I was looking for could only be found within.

How open is the aperture of our lens of perception? I know that any day I live can become dreadfully dull if I haven't tuned my fundamental state of being to the love that provides my breath, unasked and almost always, unnoticed. It's that connection, that I return to consciously in meditation, bringing me into wholeness.

Picture this: A follow spot picks out a plaintive boy soprano standing alone downstage. In the purest tones, 'Where is love?' he asks, and if it comes from the sky. He's innocently working the shmaltzy highlight of a popular musical. Is it only a shared (if attractive) delusion? Always out there. Am I really not whole, unless I'm partnered …? If he looked into a mirror, he'd be accused of narcissism, wouldn't he?

Love then, not so much as the self, but found when the self is reunited with the deepest source that is the foundation of all being.

When I lived in LA, I used to go to talks by Marianne Williamson (who later would throw her hat into the ring as a hopeful for the US Presidential battle). Marianne's teaching derives from her long-term study of *A Course in Miracles*. She teaches that 'There is nothing that any of us can do, there's nowhere that any of us can go, to make us any closer to love, *because love is who we are*. The problem is how often we think and act in ways that are not who we are.

Meanwhile, my beloved teacher Prem, with his usual adroitness, tells a story that tickles my sense of humour: Two men meet up while travelling. One of them is a thief, in hiding, the other a well-to-do businessman, who is obviously loaded. The thief turns on the charm and tags along for the ride and they share accommodation for a couple of nights, *en route*. The businessman pays for dinner.

The thief is obsessed with bagging the businessman's money and takes every chance he can get to check out the other guy's baggage, briefcase, whatever. Each night, while the other man sleeps, the thief extends his search right down to the very clothes he has been wearing. When the rich man goes to the bathroom to shower and change clothes, he even checks the pyjamas.

Where the heck does he hide the wallet?

The thief is very engaging company (he's a professional!) and they become friends. Finally, when they reach the destination where the rich guy alights to go home, the thief makes his confession: 'Look, I have to confess I'm a thief. And just out of professional interest, may I ask where you hid your wallet.'

'Oh, that's easy,' says the not-so-foolish rich man, who has enjoyed the professional's charming company, 'Each night I hid it under *your* pillow!'

When a person – gay, straight, mixed, lesbian, neither, none, but *human* (not '*homo* sexual', but *homo sapiens*) – has learned separation as a basic state of being, he or she might not have the fare to travel home. Where is that reliable home base, after all? So many places have I had to call home, in all my travels, I've been the hermit crab living in borrowed digs. When I was travelling as an instructor, I had no home base except at my Teacher's calling, wherever, whenever he brought me back to him. I always felt at home then. That essential embrace as something felt, rather than constructed.

When I was traveling on behalf of my Teacher, my darling mother would sometimes call me to come visit her, back in Perth, and I wrote this (rather cold-hearted) poem for her:

> A part of me was never born
> > still floats in amniotic bliss …
> If I laugh when you call me, Mother:
> > 'Come home' … I'm always home!
> Heart is where the home is, Ma.

Not that I ever sent her a copy, and I doubt if my darling devoted mother would have accepted these sentiments easily. But living out of a suitcase, for years, traipsing from town to town, country to country, my centre was always within, rather than being locked into one specific geographical location, or another. I would have lost my true bearings by relying too much on the externals.

Perth

November 2017 Transit lounge, Dubai airport

I'm on my way back to Perth, where I plan to settle. I grabbed some of the proceeds from the sale of my apartment in Ocean Shores to travel to Portugal to give what I hoped would be the last conference paper stemming from my academic work. The theme of the Lisbon conference was 'Representations of 'Home', which resonated strongly with my personal pre-occupations and I eventually scored another journal publication stemming from that conference.

I took the chance to go via London, where I was able to stay with old friends that I had made in Byron. After the conference I had planned to stay with an English couple in the south of Portugal where I thoroughly enjoyed the locale and their kind hospitality. As an extra bonus, after I had booked the tickets, my beloved Teacher announced an event in Barcelona and these dear friends helped me swing by Barcelona where, by some good fortune, I snagged one of the last tickets to the event.

Hence, I was immune to the crowded discomforts of travel on the flight back to Perth out of London, which was routed through Dubai.

A married couple from South Africa are connecting with the flight to Perth and are sitting right next to me in the wait lounge in Dubai. The chap is soon expressing his displeasure that he is going to a country where the (long-winded) campaign for marriage equality has just succeeded in legislation being passed in Federal Parliament to allow same-sex partnerships equal status in law. He is particularly offended that a sitting MP had used the occasion to propose marriage to his male partner, who was seated in the public gallery.

I am mildly amused at this chap's disgruntlement and I inform him that, ironically, he happens to be seated next to one of the early proponents of such an historical shift, as I had brought together testimonials from a wide range of people affected by the prejudicial *status quo*, way back in 2011 and a former, well-respected Justice of the

High Court of Australia had written a Foreword for the collection, *Speak Now*.

While I haven't given the book much attention in the intervening years, the various testimonies collected in the collection have continued to act as a useful resource, especially as several universities have included it on reading lists for various courses on offer. What a coincidence that we strangers should connect, in an airport transit lounge in 2017.

I leave the chap stewing as we board the flight.

If you think that the battle(s) have all been won, as a condescending reviewer of my book on Isherwood suggested back in 2010, you only need to look to the ongoing persecution of these people in so many countries across the world. Even closer to home, let me include these two recent events in my own life …

I am invited to a restaurant to join in the birthday celebrations of a friend of my sister. The guest of honour is rather well off, and she has booked the entire restaurant for the evening and covered the costs of the food herself. (I am not often present on such splendid occasions!)

After sharing a toast of celebratory sparkling wine in the entrance, we are seated at tables randomly throughout the space. I have met one or two other guests seated at my table, but the woman sitting to my left is unknown to me.

When we start a conversation, she asks me what work I do. I bring up my studies for the PhD and the book that I have just had published, *The Boy in the Yellow Dress*.

'Oh, what's that about?' she asks politely.

There's an imperceptible freeze around the table. The others start to pay close attention to us.

'Well, it's about growing up as a sissy boy in Perth, in the 1950s, and how I survived that hostile setting,' I say. 'It took me quite a few years to pull it together and it was part of the writing for the doctorate I was awarded back in 2006. It's called *The Boy in the Yellow Dress*, and it was published in 2014.'

'Oh, are you, um, gay? The word is poisonous and difficult for her, but I can see she's trying to be polite in this social setting. I can see too that she wants to be tolerant, but she comments, en passant:

'Oh yes, that's all right,' she says, 'but I just don't approve of your lifestyle.'

I take a breath. 'Really? Have we ever met? What do you know about my life?' (Where do they get this attitude?) 'And by the way, it's my life, not a life *style*.'

I have learned how to behave in mixed society and I'm all too practised at swallowing my truth, but my sense of self has been through a long healing process, and the residue of shame will no longer rule me. I'm not going to shout, nor embarrass this woman; but I will speak. So I continue the discussion in a calm and steady voice.

She says: 'Oh, you should really come to our church. We accept everyone …' (so that's where, all too predictably, she has derived her twisted attitude.)

I ask her: 'Is that the same place where you are taught to think in stereotypes?'

I know she is offering me an olive leaf but I've grown beyond the protocols of paranoia and I need to assert a different vision, beyond the discomfort of being 'tolerated', to a place where she can recognise the value of my lived experience and actually witness my hard-won dignity with respect.

'Oh, I know that God loves you.' Here comes the patronising smile. That's nice, isn't it.

'Who is this God that you can say that, as if you can speak for him? … And I presume it is a *him*?'

'I think you have misunderstood me,' she offers. 'I think perhaps I should move to another table.' And I agree …

And the second example?

In April 2021 I'm waiting at a bus stop after shopping for groceries. I'm not far from home but I need to conserve energy for a final push up the hill that I'll have to do on foot. A well-built man approaches me and engages me in conversation. He crosses the footpath and sits close, next to me on the bench. Why does he sit so close? with our legs touching at the thigh. When we board the bus he continues to do just that. Sits a little too close to me, as if the bus were crowded.

I think he's probably American; his name is Jerome and he's wearing the kind of cap you might see on the head of a Marine on furlough. He's bristlingly straight, but he wants to talk about yoga philosophy! So, I engage him cautiously and the conversation continues aboard the bus. He can't be coming on to me, but I can feel the questioning circling towards the inevitable inquiry: 'Are you gay?' Instinctively I feel I am being set up.

When it does indeed come up, I tell him that I'm actually *'post* gay', if anything.

He finds this intriguing. But I'm not using it as a lure. What would I do with this hunk, after all; and there's always the risk …

He needs to get off after my stop but continues his curious interrogation for the next couple of hours via text messages.

There are situations I know of where a 'gay' man gets bashed by a 'straight' guy who likes to lead him on before ultimately asserting his superior masculinity with his fists. So I am happy to simply shadowbox, to draw out just where he wants to go. He says that gay men are often attracted to him and that it offends him. He says he only wants to deal with the 'soul essence' of me, but he really wants to raise the issue of the attraction he says he draws from 'gay' men. He says he picked me out as 'gay' and when he works his way around to what is obviously a bit of an obsession, I remind him that he approached me, literally, and sat uncomfortably close to me at the bus stop.

I know it puzzles him for me to say: 'No, *post* gay,' especially when I let him know that I'm a grandfather. I have a grownup son. How so? Puzzled, he wants to know how such a thing could happen and I reply, 'Oh, the old-fashioned way … and we really enjoyed it!'

It just doesn't fit into his limited frame of understanding and, besides, the terminology is so outmoded. I tried to bring up the issue at a conference in California, asking if it was time to withdraw the term 'gay' as an identifier, much to the alarm of the American organisers who appeared to be clinging to that label.

When I submitted a paper to their collection of essays on Isherwood I used the term 'queer' about the writer. But a peer reviewer asked that

I reconsider. It's not a favoured term in the US, but I didn't think it was necessary to change it because Isherwood used that term for himself. Next to 'queer', terminology such as 'gay' seems a little epicene.

I remember the long battle taken on by activists to get the revered *New York Times* to finally give up using the term 'homosexual', replacing it with 'gay' as the term favoured by the putative 'community' that their journalists were trying to get a handle on. A victory of sorts, I suppose, but long since out of date. And what about the unwieldy LGBTQIA+ which only makes me giggle today?

So, what are we talking about if we are trying to create a class of people based on their sexual practices? The author Gore Vidal said that 'homosexual' referred to certain sexual acts, but not to a type of person. And who am I then, if I haven't had sex for years? What usefully remains of that classification? Is my identity all about sex?

It's like a cat and mouse game, and obviously Jerome thinks that he's the cat. At one point, when he is talking about his Scorpio nature, he claims that this makes him 'sensitive' to covert intentions. He is assuming that if I am 'gay' I will perforce be coming on to him. I tell him that I am 'sensitive' too, and it's not difficult for me to identify when people want to drive me back into the cave of shame and I am quite comfortable refusing that invitation!

I'm glad to find myself responding from a stronger place without being obnoxious and I tell him, if he really wants to talk about Yoga philosophy, the door is always open. What I have been engaged with for 50 years or so is part of 'Yoga' ...

But Jerome never does take up the invitation.

Snow on the roof

What, in ill thoughts again?
Men must endure their going hence even as their coming hither.
Ripeness is all. Come on.

Edgar, in Wm. Shakespeare's *King Lear*, Act 5 Scene 2

I played that character, Edgar, in an amateur production of Shakespeare's powerful tragedy, in Perth when I was in my early twenties. Disguised as Mad Tom, Edgar has been leading his father (Gloucester) around, after being brutally blinded by the bad guys. Edgar disguises his true identity to care for his dad, who wants to find his way to the highest cliff in Dover, where he might be contemplating suicide.

I cried on stage in every performance when Lear dies, after the loss of Cordelia and his precious Fool, his former greatness all destroyed by his own hubris. The classic tragic scenario, according to Aristotle, but Crikey! It still works, centuries later. Is there something in this pattern that is coded for typical brain functioning?

Now I've returned to my so-called 'hometown', after 50+ years' spent more or less running away from a palpable feeling of suffocating, but with a totally different understanding, now, of what 'home' might feel like, in a world of constant change. That stifling feeling that drove me away in my twenties seems to have dissipated altogether and I actually like the place now.

I must have cleared a lot of junk from my trunk, for I feel kindness coming at me from many sides. I've moved into a unit in a retirement village (that I'm not permitted to call 'an old folks' home' by the friends I've started making here, by the way). I'm in the 'Independent Living Unit' and can come and go as I will. I shop for myself and try to prepare my own meals. I can shut the door and be totally private or mingle when the situation presents itself. Not a bad pad for writing, in fact.

It's a little spooky to recall that when I was in the second grade in primary school (age six going on seven) that bristly teacher, Miss Watts – she of thick hair chopped short, nylon-stockinged legs that swished when she walked, and those fearsome false teeth – told us a story that has been tucked away somewhere in the back of my memory. And now it comes forwards for my attention.

I can only remember the bare bones of the story, but it had something to do with a little boy who goes away for the longest time and, through a lot of far-flung wanderings, grows old. Finally, when he returns from his worldly peregrinations, Lo! he finds peace in his own back yard. Well, fancy that! (I'm starting to sound like my Yankee grammaw.)

I resist accepting the idea for the longest time but, as one of the things I am learning to accept, it seems to have some truth to it, Dammit! Surrender seems to be the name of the game. Can you guess what's coming next? I was going to call this section 'The flight of Eros', or more bluntly, 'Life after sex' and I remember a proverb that I've only ever heard used in North America, which I may have taken the wrong way. I remember it as 'When there's snow on the roof, there's no fire down below.' And I take it as meaning 'When old age shows up (as white hair), you can be sure there's no energy in the … ahem! genital area.' I used to think that a more appropriate saying would be 'The spirit is willing, but the flesh is weak.' And I know I'm turning the original meaning of that saying on its head. It was originally about abjuring sexual activity in favour of turning towards holy matters, and the pull of sex was too strong to live a 'holy' life of renunciation. Personal experience is an uncomfortable reminder of that situation.

But no, I've been thinking that, while a part of me occasionally still yearns, albeit feebly, for intimate contact, my body doesn't respond. In other words, I can't get an erection.

Yes, I *should* call this chapter 'Life after Sex'. Besides, none of the lithe, muscled younger men with whom I would like to have taken a tumble have shown any interest in me and my aging body in many a long year. And I've never had the funds to be a 'sugar daddy'. That's a blessing. Luckily, the power of that drive has all but petered out … or been re-distributed.

Sigh. I had better get used to it. Perhaps now I can find out what lies beyond this passing, for these days I actually feel relieved to be excused from the complications and the effort required to lure one into my web! Has the dogged perseverance of all those years of meditation practice finally brought my remaining energies to the higher chakras, in a mysterious and subtle natural alchemy? What I longed for in my monk-ish days can now perhaps come true, right? I wonder if this might be too late to prove useful? Perhaps it's simply a necessary stage in getting ready to die.

Don't worry, I'm not depressed; I am facing that eventuality with a more sanguine attitude as the inevitable signs of aging manifest. (More snow on the roof.) And the space remaining leaves consciousness a calmer space. It might be a no-sex zone, hardly even the desire, but the compensations could prove rewarding.

Am I really ready to let go to that ultimate surrender? There have been distinct signs of resistance to the inevitability of age-related 'decline'. For example, I have located a good Tai Chi school here in Perth and attend classes three times per week. It's the perfect, gentle form of exercise for someone in his late seventies. Even better, I have found a very good acupuncturist, a Chinese woman who emigrated here with her husband from Shanghai, and who was trained for eight years in all aspects of Oriental medicine, and she worked in hospitals for twelve years. Her name is Helen He, and her husband's name is Jay. He is a FiFo worker in the mining industry and she cares for their two children back at home in Perth, with the help of her mother-in-law. She has it all over me, speaking several more languages than I have ever commanded. (In Paris, my antique French brings indulgent smiles to the faces of the locals.) But we have fun and form a warm friendship.

'I've always wanted to go to Shanghai', I tell her. 'Now I don't need to go there, you have come to me!' And we enjoy a fragmentary exchange of useful phrases as I revive some of the rudimentary Mandarin that I was coached in, on my frequent visits to Taiwan.

Nobody has ever needled me so accurately! In one session she was needling a point in my lower leg when my foot nearly jumped off the table and kicked her in the head.

'Wow! What was *that* point?' I ask her.

'That's the longevity point,' she replies.

'Crikey! If I keep coming to see you, I'll live to be one hundred.'

In her gentle, modest tone she corrects me: 'One hundred and twenty.'

I can tell I'm not going to be allowed to accept all the clichés about age. And my beloved Teacher Prem must have seen the early signs of conventional expectations about aging beginning to cluster in my mind, rather than my body. He rooted them out a couple of years back, when he said: 'Age is just a number!' I think I was getting ready, unconsciously, to curl up and prepare for the inevitable, after finishing a major project. But perhaps I just needed a rest.

He does have the knack of nipping nonsense in the bud. On another occasion he says: 'If you find yourself slowing down, don't worry; you were supposed to be going slower.' So I accept the company of the other old cronies where I live and join in the mutual imperative to enjoy living day by day. One day at a time … 'Long may we live and thrive!' That could turn into a manic drive to cram in as much experience as humanly possible, but I have long since learned that the quality of experience is at least as important as the quantity and, notwithstanding my straitened resources, that quality of pure enjoyment comes directly from what I tap into in my daily meditation practices, a better alternative, with a better outcome, than seeking outside for stimulation.

I made another attempt at reviving wrong-headed notions when I told my friend Anne Di Lauro, a Jungian therapist in Brisbane, that I was going to write this section and title it 'The Flight from Eros'.

'You're using Eros in the Freudian sense,' Anne tells me. 'Jung used it in a broader sense, to mean relating or connecting. Relating to friends. Relating to Spirit, even.'

This is quite striking for me, because now that I have been living in the never-to-be-called 'old' folks' home for a few years, I do feel love for many of the people here, including old ladies with white hair that I certainly would never have thought of as objects of interest! But I can honestly say I love them; or less patronisingly, that Love includes them, too.

So, 'Eros' has less to do with desire than I have assumed? Sorry, I'm a slow learner. Give me a few more years and I might understand life a little better and clear the mental vision so that the gifts of this stage of life might present, without fear (or condescension) and with deepening understanding.

Meanwhile, with signs of impending fragility appearing on a hopefully distant, or at least receding horizon, I offer up this regimen of Tai Chi, plus twice-monthly acupuncture treatments, in addition to healthy eating, trying to get enough sleep (with herbal aids!) and other acts of resistance, such as skin cancer checks and fibrous aids to move the stools! A friend here has just had both knees replaced. Another now has an artificial shoulder and at least two stents in her heart (I remember when we did this very story on stents on *Beyond 2000* as some kind of futurist fantasy!) Now she is having an actual valve replaced in her heart via a similar procedure, via a vein in her leg! Who knew such things were possible?

Notably, I have been plagued with regrets, alas! Is this inevitable, at this time of life, and will it pass? Every tiny little incident – in addition to the major ones – where I didn't act from kindness, insists on presenting itself for my consideration whenever I sit to find my peace in meditation. Memory doesn't serve me well when I'm trying to recall a name that keeps slipping away; so why does it insist on remembering all the embarrassing stuff? And how long will this dredging-up process continue?

Stronger than regret is *remorse*. I find strength in a line from the movie *Benediction*: 'Mourning the past is to begrudge the future'. In other words, recognise the lesson and resist the invitation to linger there in the shadow life and miss the opportunity for new learning, even as this ageing continues.

I had better work to find my balance and stick with that forever discipline. Yes, there's a satisfaction in the middle of my frustration. For, if I've been struggling to see beyond the limits of perception and started to track the falling away of physical stamina and endurance all the way through to decay, I am forced to ask if I am relying on the wrong instrument, the physical brain, with its electrical and chemical processes that produce thought? Is the dwindling of my *telomeres* inevitable? Have they discovered a drug that will reverse that decline, repair the drooping *telomeres*? Better to notice if there might be a way to see otherwise, using a different method?

I once visited an exhibition of painting by Taoist artists and, alongside the pictures was posted a provocative suggestion posed in Taoist terms; it went something like this: 'Better than looking with the eye, is to see (or look?) with the mind. Better than seeing with the mind is to see with your *chi*.' And, without trying to be obscure, it simply suggests to my understanding that if the body (the eye) is only seeing to a certain depth, then observing with the mind (with language, in fact), is also trying to grasp what the artist sees so profoundly (and directly) with my limited tools as well ...

I do recall that I got a clue about this from the Buddhist monk on the mountainside of Yang Ming Shan, outside of Taipei, when all those years back he chastised me: 'Aha! Don't attach!' The hint being that the lens of perception is out of balance, in an 'error of parallax'. I think he was urging me to discover the principle of equanimity – which I see now operates on several levels – out of a centre of deep stillness. Not attraction (grasping), nor rejection (pushing away). Staying in an eternal centre that is insisting on my attention these days more than ever before. That doesn't feel like a discipline, it's necessary, and it frees up my sense of being to renew what I have too lazily been calling my 'self' and allow it to grow, even as the body perceptibly fails.

Astronomers extend the reach of a telescope's range of vision, by linking up with a network of scopes in different places around the globe – all linked together to form what is, in effect a gigantic dish – to look back deeper into space (and time) to pursue their study of black holes, for example.

But I reckon that maybe the way you look determines what you can see; in effect, the instrument creates the phenomenon, and so on. I can use my intellectual capacity to try to understand the world I'm in; but it's a fine-tuning of my own sensing apparatus, my own nervous system, sitting here in stillness, that seems to be coming to the fore now.

Finally, all I can strive for is a rigorous authenticity; yes, with others, but especially with regards to myself, within my personal zone, my actual field of responsibility, to engage the life-tested clarity to win the war between clarity and confusion before the chariot, inevitably, fails.

So, to sum up … What have I been whining about? I've made a resolution lately to resume looking in the mirror to get a true fix on the testimony of the aging body. Maybe I'll learn to respect and appreciate its long service. A friend tells me: 'Alright, my body is aging around me; I am still me' and she refuses to descend into the slough of despond.

What has shifted my negative mindset is a memory that has popped up (this one in very good timing). I once went for a checkup in a hospital on the Gold Coast, trying to track down what was happening with an irregular heartbeat (a 'ventricular ectopic beat' – don't worry, that has cleared up!)

One thing that happens during the examination: notwithstanding their fancier machines, finally they sit me down with a simple ultrasound that scans a live image of my heart in black and white (and shades of grey!) in real time. There's a small flap of skin/tissue, opening and closing; a live image of my very own heart valve in operation. I am moved to realise that this simple flap – unobtrusive, unnoticed, and certainly un-thanked – has been doing its thing from the very beginning, and it is still doing so, all these decades later. I felt it at the time, and I feel it now in the recall: a small secret, disclosed in private. From a place of quiet observation there has grown the beginning of appreciation and simple gratitude in a lifetime of ignorance.

Could this be love?

I'm planning a break at Yanchep, a cosy beach town some 56 kms north of the city of Perth, to spend a couple of days re-capturing my childhood love of sunbathing and swimming in the brisk waters of the Indian Ocean. I'm staying with a dear friend, Gail Sturrock, and her mum Joy who lives nearby and both are very generous hosts.

It's just a few days after Christmas, close to New Year's Day, and there are families galore deploying a greater array of beach-going gear than we ever thought necessary in the great outdoors when we were young. Like the memorable Christmas Day way back when I was just a kid and the temperature rose to 109 degrees Fahrenheit and our entire family went to the beach for the day. No sunscreen, no hats, no umbrellas, just a slow broiling in the sun.

I visit the Skin Cancer Council shop in Subiaco and grab their last sunproof hat that fits me; one with a sensibly wide brim, plus something called a 'rashie', with long sleeves. These both have a high SPF factor to protect my skin from the possibilities of sunburn. I've learned the hard way as a result of an earlier bout of shingles, that skin that has been rendered vulnerable to such assaults doesn't take kindly to sunburn. And that sensitivity can cut down the number of hours spent on the beach.

I am well prepared ... or so I think.

The sunlight is strong and the mood is balmy. I resort to one of the family-safe areas – at Fisherman's Hollow, just around from the lagoon itself – wearing the protective long-sleeved rashie and the invulnerable hat. I take up my space on the beach among some rocky outcrop, in case the wind freshens, and I lose myself in the memory of basking.

I remember that the wind here shifts around to a southerly, too early sometimes, and my basking will have to be brought short, so I wade into the cool water of this cosy little family beach, pushing through a strange current that is running rapidly to the north, absurdly close along the shoreline. I get caught in this unusual current and as insignificant as it has seemed, I quickly lose my strength by resisting its power, with the buoyancy of the stupid rashie keeping my feet from touching base on the bottom. As I try to cross it and reach a place where I can establish a foothold, it keeps forcing me up close to the sharp-edged rock at the edges of the reef that encloses the lagoon.

Families play at the shoreline, oblivious to my embarrassment and my loss of personal competency.

When my strength has gone, and resistance is obviously pointless, I am forced to recognise that I need to find help. I'm a grown man and I would feel mortified to call 'lifesavers' to me. Besides, the lifesavers' tower is around the bend and out of sight on this bland, fine day.

Humiliation is known as the process of being humbled and I feel plain stupid. No room here for a male ego-trip. I call mutely for help to my blessed guru and guide, even while wondering, how could He reach me here? Meditation is difficult *in extremis* and I wonder how my lifelong Teacher could come to my rescue now, today, in this beach setting, in Western Australia on a hot early summer day. 'Leave no room for doubt in your mind' is one his oldest pieces of advice.

But my energy has faded, and I can't stand up.

Just then a sturdy young woman comes swimming by ... Her head is submerged, viewing the ocean floor through frogperson's goggles, and she's breathing through a snorkel arrangement. Luckily, she comes up and notices me. Despite my embarrassment, I have no option but to ask her:

'Can you ... *gulp* ... help me?' Crikey, that was hard to do.

She has found her footing and without hesitating reaches out to grab each of my hands in hers and pulls me to a standing position. I am intensely relieved. But as soon as she releases her grip, I fall backwards into the same absurdly helpless position. The effort I have expended over the past ten minutes or so has weakened the muscles in my 76-year-old neck and back.

She doesn't hesitate to grab my hands again and starts to pull me towards the shore, her eyes locked onto mine. Two young men come forward, recognising some need in my enfeebled stagger and she passes me on to them. The men grab hold of an arm each and, with what soon becomes the standard inquiry, 'Are you alright?' look into my eyes.

They walk me to my towel. I stand there unsteadily, still feeling the weakness pulling me backwards. I feel intensely embarrassed and scarcely able to stand, given my physical exhaustion, when another young woman, another stranger, comes up, saying 'Are you alright?' bless her.

'Do you need some water?'

I try to gather some dignity and assure her that I have some water in my car, 'just up these steps', as I try to steady myself. I just want to get away from the scene of my humiliation. In my weakened state, the metal stairway up to the carpark is quite a challenge, so if I should happen to fall, it will provide only a hard-edged, brutal landing place. But she recognises something of the vestiges of male pride as she looks into my eyes, and she proceeds to climb the steps, immediately behind me, just in case I need help, bless her again! I take it one step at a time, gripping on each and every upright as I head up the stairway.

I am relieved to reach the car, and I thank her, deeply humbled, calling her an angel of mercy. Each one of these rescuers has been a stranger but, as they have stepped forward to help me, they have all responded from the bottom line of some common humanity; and that look – peering deep into my face, past my embarrassment – is curiously impersonal, looking past the point of everyday social communication to reach me.

'Are you alright?'

If my guru has heard my whimper for help, I realise that He reached me from that place of common humanity, so evident, so spontaneous in the face and eyes of each of these strangers.

Full circle

When all is said, and done, (and written), the boy in the yellow dress has travelled a long and circuitous road to find his way home. But that home, as he realised halfway, was not a physical, geographic location. Although it's a sweet and highly symbolic story that he travelled all over the planet to come back to the place where his body landed all those decades ago, it was with him all the while. It was/is mobile; always hidden within the mysteries of breathing.

Although I am learning to respect its essential needs, I know this body will drop away, eventually, sooner or later, when its work is done. It's not the be-all and end-all. If everything is always changing and what has a beginning will always come to an end, there has been this constant presence, even when I was hardly paying attention to it at all.

Acknowledgements

Heartfelt thanks to Amanda Lohrey, Ruth Blair, Lee Dunn, Valerie Marsh, and the wonder woman Kaite Hansen, who insisted that this all should be written about in the first place. To Laurence Browne, Anne Di Lauro and Dr Chris Morgan who gave such thoughtful readings of this manuscript at different stages.

Gordon Thompson, the courageous independent publisher of Clouds of Magellan Press who has published four of my books with generous and far-sighted patience. Gordon and his impressive wife Petrina Barson showed me a different kind of progressive Christianity that helped lift the toxic cloud of prejudice from me. And thanks also to Helen Bell, editor at Clouds of Magellan Press, for sensitive reading and astute editing across four titles.

Gillian Whitlock, Ruth Blair and Veny Armanno at UQ, who saw something worth supporting in my eccentric and half-formed research plans.

Peter Abbott and Johnny Young, each of whom gave me a job when I really needed it. And at FOX and Paramount Studios, that true mensch Ron Vandor for his support.

Kim O'Leary and Geoff Bridgford for their friendship and the unique musical genius that each manifests. Their heart songs are the manifestation of peace, bless them.

Dr Simon LeVay, Susan Peters, George Meyer, Greg Vogel and Susie Witten as my allies in Los Angeles.

Richard Sattler as my wicketkeeper for the timely Hollywood fact-checking.

Gail Sturrock for generously providing a space for me to work on a late draft of the manuscript.

And, beyond words, Dave Lawrence for his wise and compassionate forgiveness.

Bibliography

Benediction. 2021. Reiver Pictures, dir. Terence Davies.

Bhikkhu, Thanissaro. *The Buddhist Monastic Code I: The Pāṭimokkha Rules Translated and Explained by Thanissaro Bhikkhu.* Thanissaro Bhikkhu, 1994.

Benedict, Ruth. *Patterns of Culture.* Houghton Mifflin, 1934.

Blain, Jenny. Wallis, Robert Wallis. 'The 'Ergi' Seidman: contestations of gender, shamanism and sexuality in Northern religion past and present'. *Journal of Contemporary Religion* 2000 15.3.

Campbell, Joseph, and Bill Moyers. *The Power of Myth.* Edited by Betty Sue Flowers. Anchor Books, 1991.

Dalziell, Rosamund. *Shameful Autobiographies: Shame in Contemporary Australian Autobiographies and Culture.* Melbourne University Press, 2018.

Dragoin, William. 'The Gynemimetic Shaman: Evolutionary origins of male sexual inversion and associated talent.' In *Gender Blending.* Eds. Bonnie Bullough, Vern L Bullough & James Elias. Prometheus Books, 1997.

Thích Nhat Hanh, *Interbeing: The 14 Mindfulness Trainings of Engaged Buddhism* (4th ed.), Parallax Press, 2020.

Harvey, Andrew. *The Way of Passion: A Celebration of Rumi.* North Atlantic Books, 1994.

Isherwood, Christopher. *My Guru and His Disciple.* Farrar, Straus and Giroux, 1980.

Jung, CG. *Collected Works.* Princeton University Press.

Ungunmerr-Baumann, Miriam-Rose. 'Dadirri: Official Miriam Rose Ungunmerr Baumann Video.' House of Listening, 17 Dec. 2020, https://www.house-of-listening.com/blog/dadirri-official-video

McClure, John A. *Partial Faiths: Postsecular Fiction in the Age of Pynchon and Morrison.* University of Georgia Press, 2007.

Merton, Thomas. *The Way of Chuang Tzu.* New Directions, 1965.

Walter Williams, *The Spirit and the Flesh: Sexual Diversity in American Indian Cultures.* Beacon Press, 1992.

Watts, Alan. *The Way of Zen.* Pantheon Books, 1957

Mr Isherwood Changes Trains by Victor Marsh

British expatriate writer Christopher Isherwood (1904-1986) moved to America prior to the Second World War and lived more than half his life in California, writing for the Hollywood studios. Famous initially for the stories he wrote during the rise of the Nazis, he attracted a second wave of interest in the 1970s with his 'out' autobiography *Christopher and His Kind* (1976). But much less is known about Isherwood's writing during his forty years as a student of a guru from the Ramakrishna Order.

In *Mr Isherwood Changes Trains*, Victor Marsh interrogates the assumptions and prejudices that have combined to disparage the sincerity of Isherwood's religious life. Marsh elucidates those features of Vedanta philosophy that enabled Isherwood to integrate the various aspects of his dharma: his vocation as a writer, and a spirituality not predicated on the repudiation of his sexuality. Marsh details the heartfelt search for a 'home-self' that found expression in later works such as *My Guru and his disciple* and in what is seen as Isherwood's finest novel, *A single man*.

Speak Now: Australian Perspectives on Same-Sex Marriage
ed. Victor Marsh

A collection of essays, reflections and personal stories from 'enthusiasts, acceptors, sceptics and hesitants' showing the passion and depth around the issue of same-sex marriage. Over thirty writers, a mix of activist and reflective voices, explore the legacy of the 2004 changes to the Australian *Marriage Act*, which now states – and which must be stated at every wedding* – 'marriage is between a man and a woman'. **Marriage Equality was brought into Australian law in 2017.*

The Boy in the Yellow Dress by Victor Marsh

Perth in the 1950s. After being caught wearing his mother's yellow dress, young Victor had to hide any tendency towards gender inappropriate behaviour. But his interest in dancing and theatre (and mooning over Rudolph Nureyev on the telly) were bound to make the façade collapse at some point. Emerging sexuality and the sense of not being 'at home' in his body, let alone the world, ran alongside a search for meaning that brought him eventually to a spiritual awakening under the young guru Maharaji …

Part family tragedy, part existential comedy, *The Boy in the Yellow Dress* is a warts-and-all account of exile and the subsequent journey homewards that is less about finding a respectable place in the world than an intimate connection with the ultimate source of being.

If ever a memoir captured the Zeitgeist, it's this one … Wise, funny, surprising at every turn … More than a portrait of growing up gay, it chronicles the wild search for meaning of an entire generation. Amanda Lohrey

My Teacher's Name is Love – Some Poems for Prem by Victor Marsh

A collection of poems examining love, self, devotion, and opening to a wider cosmos. Whimsical, meditative, rapturous, these poems are a contemporary expression of spirit.

www.ingramcontent.com/pod-product-compliance
Lightning Source LLC
Chambersburg PA
CBHW040253170426
43191CB00019B/2392